GRAND TETON
TRIVIA

CHARLIE CRAIGHEAD

RIVERBEND
PUBLISHING

To Bert Raynes,
who has forgotten more trivia
than I'll ever know.

Grand Teton Trivia

Copyright © 2009 by Charlie Craighead

Published by Riverbend Publishing, Helena, Montana

ISBN 13: 978-1-60639-009-2

Printed in the United States of America.

2 3 4 5 6 7 8 9 0 MG 15 14 13

Cataloging-in-Publication data is on file at the Library of Congress.

Cover design by Bob Smith
Text design by Barbara Fifer

Riverbend Publishing
P.O. Box 5833
Helena, MT 59604
1-866-787-2363
www.riverbendpublishing.com

Contents

GEOLOGY &
GEOGRAPHY

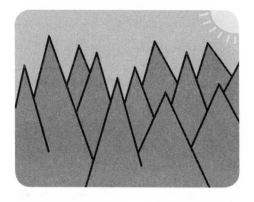

Q. What is the Teton Range?
A. A relatively small but spectacular mountain range in the northwest corner of Wyoming, just south of Yellowstone National Park. The Teton Range is part of the Rocky Mountains.

Q. How large is the Teton Range?
A. About 40 miles long and 10 to 15 miles wide, or roughly half the size of Long Island, New York.

Q. How tall are the Tetons?
A. They rise almost 7,000 feet above the Jackson Hole valley to an elevation of more than 13,000 feet above sea level.

Q. What is the tallest peak?
A. The Grand Teton is 13,770 feet above sea level.

Q. Is this the tallest peak in Wyoming?
A. No, Gannett Peak in the Wind River Range is fifteen feet taller.

Q. How old are the Tetons?
A. They are the youngest mountain range in the Rockies, formed in the last 7 to 10 million years.

Q. How old are the rest of the Rocky Mountains?
A. They are more than 50 million years old. For comparison, the Appalachian Mountains began to rise about 300 million years ago.

Q. What event initiated the rise of the Rocky Mountains?
A. A tectonic plate under the Pacific Ocean was forced under North America, crumpling the continent and forming the Rockies.

Q. What happened when this tectonic plate melted from the heat beneath North America?
A. It created volcanic activity in this area.

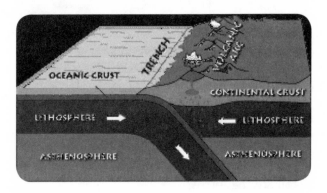

Q. What signs of this heat and plate movement are evident in the landscape surrounding the Tetons?
A. A hotspot deep in the earth powers the geysers of Yellowstone National Park. The movement also left a trail of volcanoes on the surface of the earth. Since the North American tec-

tonic plate is slowly drifting to the southwest, and the hotspot is staying in a relatively fixed spot in the earth, the volcanic trail shows up in a path heading southwest from Yellowstone, across Idaho and into Nevada. However, nothing in geology is that simple. Other evidence, including a volcanic path leading northwest from Yellowstone and the lack of proof for a deep plume of heat under the park, cause geologists to continue refining their theories.

Q. How fast is the North American Plate moving?

A. About an inch a year. So, in the average American's lifetime, the Tetons and Yellowstone will have moved about six feet in relation to the hot magma under the park.

Q. What caused the Tetons to form so much later than the rest of the Rockies?
A. Residual heat from the melting tectonic plate caused the West to rise and stretch, forming a vast landscape of mountains and valleys known as the Basin and Range Province. The Tetons formed on the eastern edge of this region as the area was stretched and fractured.

Q. Why did the Tetons form such a dramatic landscape?
A. The Teton Range rose and the Jackson Hole valley dropped along a fault that runs along the base of the present-day mountains. The lifting and lowering on opposite sides of the fault formed the Tetons, an abrupt range of peaks with no foothills.

Q. What is the name of this fault?
A. The Teton Fault.

Q. Where can evidence of the Teton Fault be clearly seen?
A. Just above String Lake there's an open hillside with a crescent-shaped scarp caused by the movement along the fault.

Q. What type of fault is it?
A. It is a "normal fault" where the actual crack or fault is a steeply angled (45 degrees or more) break in the bedrock, and the rock on the upper side of the fault slides down in relation-

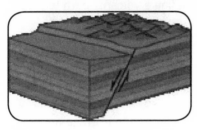

ship to the other side. Just imagine holding two similar wooden blocks tightly to- gether, one in each hand, and then sliding the one in your right hand down against the other while sliding the left one up; this is basically what happened to the Tetons (the block in your left hand) and the Jackson Hole valley (the block in your right hand). Normal faults are usually caused by the land being stretched or pulled.

Q. What phenomenon accompanies the rock slipping up and down along the fault?
A. An earthquake.

Q. What magnitude earthquake do some geologists say is over- due along the Teton Fault?
A. Up to a magnitude 7.5.

Q. How much difference is there between the rising of the mountains and the sinking of the valley?
A. More than thirty thousand feet, or five-and-a-half to six miles!

Q. What visual image do geologists use to explain how the Tetons formed?
A. Imagine a pair of giant trapdoors (imagine, of course, that they are very thick doors) in the earth—where the two doors meet in the middle is the Teton Fault. One door swings upward to form the mountains and the other swings down to form the valley

Q. If the Teton Range side of the Teton Fault and the Jackson Hole valley side moved almost six miles up and down in relation to each other, then why do the Teton peaks today stand only a mile and a half above the valley floor?

A. Most of the offset along the fault, about 20,000 feet, came in the sinking of the valley. The rest came in the rising of the mountains. But remember, it took millions and millions of years for the offset to occur along the fault; it didn't move 30,000 feet in one big earthquake, so the mountains were getting eroded even as they rose up. Also, the valley filled in with glacial rock and debris over the millennia to make the flat valley we see in front of the Tetons now, covering up the steeply-angled, original bedrock that sank along the fault. If you were to try to match up the original points where the two sides of the landscape fit together before the Teton Fault was formed, you would find one point at the top of the Grand Teton and the other five miles deep in the earth at the base of the mountains. Even today, the valley floor is tilted slightly toward the mountains like the bedrock deep below.

Q. If the valley side of the "trapdoor" really sank 20,000 feet where it meets the mountains, why is the valley floor level and not steeply sloped toward the Tetons?

A. Over the millions of years it took to happen, rocky material from the surrounding area was carried by glaciers, erosion, and other means to fill the valley.

Q. When did the Tetons stop rising?

A. They didn't. They are still rising at the rate of about a foot every five hundred years. And the Jackson Hole valley is still sinking.

Q. How did the Tetons get their distinct look?

A. A combination of factors created the incredible Teton landscape. First of all, the huge vertical movement along the Teton Fault created the setting. Then water, ice, and gravity carved away at the slowly rising land. But some of the rock was more resistant to erosion and didn't wear away as fast. The high, central peaks are capped with hard granite that weathers very slowly, so they stand taller. Several Ice Ages occurred during the formation of the Tetons, and the resulting glaciers carved classic U-shaped canyons and valleys. Then the valleys filled with glacial debris to form flat bottoms in stark contrast to the abrupt rise of the mountains.

Q. Is the process finished?
A. Geology is never finished. This is an ongoing process; much of the Tetons' rugged look is due to their relatively young age. If you come back

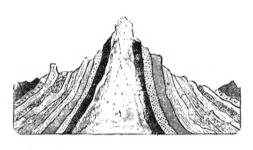

in about 40 million years, the mountains will most likely be worn down and look much older!

Q. Why aren't all the peaks in the Teton Range the same height?
A. The hardest rock—the rock most resistant to erosion—occurs in the middle of the range. This rock forms the central high peaks.

Q. What name is given to the group of mountains comprising the six central peaks of the Tetons?
A. The Cathedral Group.

Q. Are the Tetons made entirely of granite?
A. No, only the five highest peaks are largely granite. The Tetons are composed mostly of gneiss (pronounced without the "g," just like "nice"), a sugary-textured metamorphic rock formed from even older rocks. In the Tetons, gneiss looks like banded layers of light and dark rock, often folded into twisted shapes. The different bands of gneiss reflect the different rock types they once were—sedimentary and volcanic—that were heated and squeezed together deep in the earth.

Q. How deep in the earth was gneiss formed?
A. About 18 miles down.

Q. What is the name of the granite forming the highest peaks of the Tetons?

A. The formal name is Mount Owen Quartz monzonite, but generally it is just called Mount Owen Granite. Quartz monzonite is a type of granite containing two kinds of feldspar—one rich in potassium and the other rich in sodium and calcium. Up close, you can see that the Mount Owen monzonite is made of gray quartz and white feldspar, giving it an overall whitish or light gray appearance. Flecks of different colored mica give the granite a sprinkling of dark spots.

Q. What other types of rock make up parts of the Tetons?

A. Limestone and sandstone flank the central range to the west, north, and south.

Q. Where can you see a prominent example of this sandstone?

A. There is a cap of sandstone on top of Mount Moran.

Q. How did it get there?

A. Before the mountains rose, the sandstone was on top of the gneiss that now forms Mount Owen. The sandstone survived being lifted and eroded as the Tetons formed. The same rock can be found east of the park, near the "hinge" of the trapdoor we imagine to explain the mountains' rise.

Q. What are the vertical black lines that appear in some of the peaks?

A. They are called dikes, and they are made of diabase. Diabase is rock similar to basalt, and was molten at one point when the gneiss and granite of the Tetons were still deep in the earth. The molten magma was forced up into vertical cracks in the gneiss and granite before the mountains rose.

Q. When did this happen?

A. About 765 million years ago.

Q. How wide is the diabase dike on Mount Moran?

A. 150 feet.

Q. What natural phenomenon of climate was largely responsible for the present-day appearance of the Tetons?
A. The Ice Ages.

Q. When did they occur?
A. Beginning about two million years ago, there have been about 12 periods of glaciation in the Teton area.

Q. When was the last major period of glapciation in the park?
A. It began roughly 50,000 years ago and ended just 14,000 years ago.

Q. What was the last period of glaciers called?
A. The Pinedale Period.

Q. What cultural event overlapped with the melting of the last glaciers?
A. The arrival of humans to this area.

Q. How deep was the glacial ice in and around Jackson Hole during the Bull Lake Period about 150,000 years ago?
A. The ice was about 3,500 feet thick where it formed on the Yellowstone Plateau, and about 2,000 feet thick in the valley in front of the Tetons.

Q. What obvious present-day evidence remains of the glaciers?
A. Low ridges of soil and rock called moraines. These formed along the edges or at the ends of the glaciers.

Q. Where can some of these moraines be seen in Grand Teton National Park?
A. The curved, tree-covered hill that nestles by Phelps Lake is

a lateral moraine left by the glacier that flowed out of Death Canyon, and the forested ring around Jenny Lake is the terminal moraine of a glacier that once flowed out of Cascade Canyon.

Q. Besides their shape, how are moraines along the base of the mountains easily recognized?
A. They are usually tree-covered due to their soil, which holds more moisture and nutrients than the surrounding glacial-washed soil.

Q. How does a glacier move?
A. When more snow falls in the mountains each year than melts, the remaining snow gradually turns to ice, forming an ice field. When the ice field gets deep enough—about sixty feet thick—it begins to "flow" under its own massive weight, almost like thick plastic putty. At this point it is officially a glacier. The glacier slowly moves from higher elevations to lower elevations as long as new ice continues to form in the higher areas, adding its weight and pressure to the top of the glacier.

Q. What did the glaciers carry along with them as they flowed?
A. Lots of rocks that were either scraped up by the ice or fell on top of the ice.

Q. What happened to all those rocks?
A. They were left wherever they happened to be when the glacial ice melted. Rocks that were ground underneath the massive ice flows were rounded and polished; those carried on top of the ice remained more angular.

Q. What is an erratic?
A. A large rock that was carried along by a glacier and eventually left behind wherever the glacier melted.

Q. Where are erratics in Grand Teton National Park?
A. All along the base of the Tetons, especially visible as large

boulders in the forest around Jenny Lake and Leigh Lake.

Q. How can you tell if a large rock is an erratic?
A. Erratics often look "out of place" in their surroundings. They are usually much larger than other rocks in the immediate area and appear mostly on top of the ground rather than buried in it.

Q. At what speed does the Teton Glacier at the base of the Grand Teton move downhill?
A. 30 feet per year.

Q. What was the favorite joke response of old-timers in this area when tourists asked what happened to the glaciers?
A. "I guess they went back for more rocks."

Q. What lake bed was scoured 800 feet deep by glaciers during the last period of ice?
A. Jackson Lake. It was formed originally by the fault movement that created the Tetons, and later deepened by glaciers.

Q. How deep is the lake now?
A. After partially filling with sediment over the years, the lake is still 437 feet deep near the mountains.

Q. What is the name for the type of lake formed when a glacier scours a hole and piles up a moraine that acts like a dam?
A. A piedmont lake.

Q. Are there any piedmont lakes in Grand Teton National Park?
A. All of the lakes along the base of the Tetons are piedmont lakes.

Q. How deep is Jenny Lake, a piedmont lake at the mouth of Cascade Canyon?
A. 236 feet.

Q. What other evidence did the glaciers leave?
A. The classic U-shaped canyons of the Tetons were formed

by smaller glaciers that flowed out of the mountains and met the massive ice filling the valley, most recently about 15,000 to 20,000 years ago.

Q. When did the last of the glacial ice melt?
A. It didn't. New glaciers formed high in the Tetons between 1350 AD and 1850 AD during a cold period called the Little Ice Age. Those 12 glaciers are still here and actively carving at the peaks.

Q. What major geological event occurred in the valley from about 10 million to about 5 million years ago, before the Ice Ages?
A. Jackson Hole was submerged by a huge lake that deposited 5,000 feet of sediment.

Q. What nearby geological feature is having an effect on the Tetons?
A. The Yellowstone Hotspot, a chamber of hot magma that powers the thermal features of that park. The hotspot can melt faults or cause movement in nearby faults, including the Teton Fault.

THE MAJOR TETON PEAKS

Q. What peak was named for its frequent lightning strikes?
A. Static Peak.

Q. Which peak was named for a topographer who built a stone cairn on its summit in 1898?
A. Buck Mountain, named for George A. Buck.

Q. Which peak is named for its partially hidden position and frequent cloud cover?
A. Veiled Peak.

Q. Which peak was named after the author of the book *The Virginian?*
A. Mount Wister was named for novelist Owen Wister, a frequent visitor to the Tetons. In 1912 Wister bought a small

homestead near the JY Ranch and built a summer cabin for his family. His wife died the following year and Wister never returned.

Q. Which two peaks were named solely for their relationship to the Grand Teton?
A. South Teton and Middle Teton.

Q. What peak is named for a tribe of North American Indians who often came to the Tetons to hunt?
A. Nez Perce Peak.

Q. What name change was given to the Grand Teton in 1872?
A. It was called Mount Hayden, after expedition leader Ferdinand V. Hayden, but the name didn't stick.

Q. Which three peaks were called the Pilot Knobs by fur trappers in the early 1800s?
A. South, Middle, and Grand Teton.

Q. Why were they named that?
A. The three peaks were used as a landmark for travel because they were visible for many miles from all directions. The word "pilot" meant a guide for travelers.

Q. What did the French trappers call the same three peaks?
A. Les Trois Tetons, or "The Three Breasts."

Q. What did Native Americans call the Tetons?
A. The Hoary Headed Fathers, among other things.

Q. Which peak was named for the climber and surveyor who made the first documented climb of the Grand Teton?
A. Mount Owen, named for William "Billy" Owen.

Q. Which peak is named for the Shoshone Indian word meaning "pinnacles"?
A. Teewinot Mountain, for the Shoshone word Tee-Win-At. Apparently, though, the Shoshone applied the term to the entire Teton Range and not just to one peak.

Q. Which peak was named after a geologist on the 1872 Hayden Expedition?
A. Mount St. John, named for Orestes H. St. John.

Q. What peak was named for the many marmots that inhabit its slopes?
A. Rockchuck Peak.

Q. What peak was named for the first Superintendent of Grand Teton National Park?
A. Mount Woodring, named after Samuel T. Woodring, who launched the new national park with an ambitious program of trail building.

Q. Albright Peak is named for what person?
A. Horace Albright, an early director of the National Park Service and a proponent of expanding Grand Teton National Park to preserve the entire valley.

Q. Which peak was named after the landscape artist who first painted the Tetons?
A. Mount Moran was named for Thomas Moran, a British-born painter whose beautiful works of Yellowstone in 1871 probably tipped the balance toward creating our nation's first national park.

Q. Who first climbed Mount Moran?
A. LeGrand Haven Hardy, Ben C. Smith, and Bennet McNulty,

in 1922. These men became interested after hearing about the difficulties encountered by LeRoy Jeffers, librarian of the American Alpine Club, in his efforts to climb the peak. Jeffers and his wife attempted the peak in 1919, enduring storms and a large rock slide in their failed effort.

Q. Who first climbed Mount St. John and Teewinot Mountain?
A. Park rangers Fritiof Fryxell (pronounced Frit-ee-off Frix-ell) and Phil Smith, making the first ascents of both peaks less than a week apart, in August 1929. These two men were hired as seasonal rangers for the fledgling park but spent as much time as possible exploring and naming the peaks. They also established the system of summit registers, still in use today, that climbers use to record their ascents.

Q. What tragedy happened on Mount Moran in November 1950?
A. A DC-3 airplane carrying 21 people crashed, killing all aboard, including seven children. The plane belonged to the New Tribes Mission and was en route to South America. Witnesses saw the plane circle beneath the clouds covering Mount Moran, then climb up into the clouds where it flew directly into a large boulder just above Skillet Glacier. The pilot's log indicated they thought they were farther north, and it's assumed they had some kind of electrical failure. The victims' remains were buried at the site, and the wreckage is still there. The National Park Service requests that climbers respect the area by detouring around it.

Q. What Hollywood stars were filming in the park and heard the explosion?
A. Kirk Douglas and his 6-year-old son, Michael. Kirk was starring in the feature film, *The Big Sky*.

THE JACKSON HOLE VALLEY

Q. Teton County, Wyoming, which includes Grand Teton National Park, is 2,697,000 acres. What percent of the county is public land?
A. 97%.

Q. The Bridger-Teton National Forest, which borders Grand Teton, is the second largest national forest in the lower 48 states. How large is it?
A. 3.4 million acres, or 5,312 square miles, an area larger than the state of Connecticut (5,006 square miles).

Q. What is the elevation of the flat valley floor of Jackson Hole?
A. About 6,500 feet above sea level.

Q. Jackson is the county seat, but what small town within the park boundaries once vied with Jackson for the title?
A. Kelly.

Q. What geological event led to the demise of Kelly?
A. The Gros Ventre Slide on the north side of Sheep Mountain in 1925. ("Gros Ventre" is pronounced "Grow Vont.")

Q. What was the Gros Ventre Slide?
A. One of the world's largest landslides. It was caused by a combination of geologic factors—one rock formation lying over another at just the right angle to slide, the erosion of part of the upper  rock layer that gave it room to move, and most of all, a drenching wet spring. Homesteader William Bierer, who lived where the slide occurred, had predicted the slide for years. He said that he could hear water running underground all over the north slope of Sheep Mountain. Bierer moved away before the mountain slid.

Q. How much rock and soil slid down?
A. An estimated 50 million cubic feet. This is about the same volume as one of the twin towers of the World Trade Center that fell on September 11, 2001.

Q. What did the slide cover up?
A. It dammed the Gros Ventre River with a rock dam 225 feet high and half a mile wide, creating the five-mile-long Lower Slide Lake.

Q. How did this lead to the demise of Kelly?
A. In 1927, two years after engineers had declared it safe, the rock dam gave way and the resulting flood tore through Kelly.

Q. How many people died in the resulting flood?
A. 6 people, including all three members of the Kneedy family, who ignored warnings.

Q. Why wasn't the death toll higher?
A. Luckily the dam broke in the daytime and the townspeople were warned the flood was coming. Most were able to escape. Forty families lost their homes. Only the church and school survived. At that time Kelly had a population of 50, and it had stores, a hotel, a livery stable, and other businesses. Today it is a small residential area with one store and an elementary school.

Q. How far did the flood waters travel?
A. The town of Wilson, at the foot of Teton Pass, was flooded as the water surged south through the Snake River Canyon and into Idaho.

Q. What remnant of the flood reappeared in 1999?
A. A safe belonging to the Kneedy family was found two miles downstream in the National Elk Refuge. It was discovered partially exposed on the stream bank, and a crew returned with heavy equipment to uncover it and haul it away. The safe was opened later at a ceremony and Kneedy personal belongings were identified. Most of the contents had been destroyed by the water and mud that had leaked into the safe.

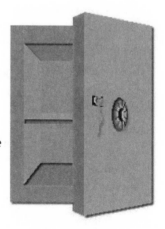

Q. What other nearby dam has failed?
A. The original Jackson Lake Dam, built in 1906-07 of log cribs

filled with rock, failed in 1910. This was before the park was established.

Q. When was the Jackson Lake Dam rebuilt?
A. From 1911 to 1916. This time it was concrete with an earthen dike.

Q. How much did this dam elevate the natural height of Jackson Lake?
A. 39 feet.

Q. The dam was found unsafe in the event of a big earthquake on the Teton Fault and it was reinforced in the late 1980s. What magnitude earthquake do engineers now say it can withstand?
A. A 7.5 magnitude quake.

Q. When did the last earthquake of that size occur along the Teton Fault?
A. Between 4,800 and 7,000 years ago.

Q. When did the last earthquake of that size occur in the Yellowstone-Teton region?
A. In 1959, when the 7.5 magnitude Hebgen Lake earthquake triggered a landslide that dammed the Madison River in Montana, killing 28 people and forming Earthquake (Quake) Lake.

Q. If the Jackson Lake Dam did fail, how long would it take the flood waters to reach park headquarters at Moose?
A. Five hours.

Q. What prominent dam in the Teton region collapsed in 1976?
A. The Teton Dam on the Teton River in Idaho, just west of Grand Teton National Park. The Teton Dam was a $100 million earthen dam, and its collapse led to the deaths of eleven people, the loss of thousands of cattle, and hundreds of millions in damages. The Teton River originates just over the Idaho/Wyoming line and gathers water from the west slope of the Tetons.

Q. How did Signal Mountain, just above the Jackson Lake dam, get its name?
A. From a signal fire that was lit during a search of the Snake River for a drowned man in 1891.

Q. Who took the first photographs from the summit of Signal Mountain?
A. William H. Jackson, in 1878. Jackson was a pioneer American photographer who traveled the West with early expeditions. He preferred landscape photography but also pho-tographed American Indians and the settling of the West.

Q. What river feeds Jackson Lake?
A. The Snake River.

Q. Why is it named the Snake?
A. Lewis and Clark named it the Lewis River, but early French trappers knew it as the Mad River. It later became known as the Snake after the Snake, or Shoshone, Indians who inhabited the area.

Q. Where does the Snake River begin?
A. In southern Yellowstone National Park.

Q. How long is the Snake River?
A. 1,056 miles, making it the tenth longest river in the country.

Q. How many feet in elevation does it drop before joining the Columbia River?
A. 9,500 feet.
Q. Yellowstone is known for its thermal features. How many warm springs occur in Grand Teton?
A. Six.

Q. What is a "hole" as in Jackson Hole?

A. It's the term used by early fur trappers for a valley sur-rounded by mountains.

Q. What was the only viable resource mined in Jackson Hole?
A. Coal.

Q. Who developed the first coal mines, and why?
A. The U.S. Reclamation Service mined coal in 1914 during construction of the Jackson Lake Dam. The mine has been shut down for many years, and no other mining is permitted within the park boundaries. Other small coal mines operated in the  area until the 1940s, but they only served locals since the cost to trans-port coal out of the valley was too great. Mineral rights in the surround-ing national forests are still open to leasing, and occasional permits are given for oil and gas exploration or for small gold mining operations.

Q. What was the valley's only real boom town?
A. Moran, near the Jackson Lake Dam. It began when Ben Sheffield built a hunting and fishing lodge on the road to Yel-lowstone near the present-day dam site. When the Bureau of Reclamation arrived to build a new dam in 1910, they built barracks, warehouses, a hospital, mess hall, and more. Other lodges and tourist facilities sprang up, and soon there were more than a hundred buildings. In 1929 the Sheffields and oth-ers sold out to the Snake River Land Company, and by 1959 all the buildings had been taken down or moved away by the Na-tional Park Service. Some of the cabins went to nearby Colter Bay. Today, Moran is a small residential area with a post office and school, re-located to the park's Moran entrance.

Q. Signal Mountain Lodge, on Jackson Lake, began life as the Ole Warner fish camp. What prominent Jackson Hole family bought it from Ole and turned it into a first-class resort?
A. The Wort family, who sold their lakeshore property in 1939 and built the Wort Hotel in Jackson.

Q. What other site in the park was built by the Wort family?
A. The Wort Boathouse on Jenny Lake, a log building listed on the National Register of Historic Places.

Q. What natural features in Grand Teton have been viewed as having the shapes of animals?
A. Nez Perce Peak, which Native Americans saw as the silhouette of a howling dog, and Blacktail Butte, which, when viewed from the north along Highway 89, looks like a rabbit asleep on its back. Sheep Mountain, just outside the park boundary, has long been known as the Sleeping Indian for the shape of a war-bonneted chief on his back.

Q. What two lakes are the oldest glacial lakes in the valley?
A. Two Ocean Lake and Emma Matilda Lake formed 20,000 to 25,000 years ago.

Q. Blacktail Butte, which looks like an island in the middle of the valley in front of the Tetons, is a remnant of what?
A. The valley bedrock that sank down on the east side of the Teton Fault.

Q. What is unique about Pacific Creek, which empties into the Snake River near Moran Junction?
A. Its source is Two Ocean Creek in the nearby Teton Wilderness. Shortly after it begins on the Continental Divide, Two Ocean Creek forks into Pacific Creek and Atlantic Creek. Pacific Creek water joins the Snake River and eventually reaches the Pacific Ocean. Atlantic Creek water ultimately finds its way to the Atlantic Ocean.

Q. How did Arizona Creek, which empties into Jackson Lake, get its name?
A. Not from the state of Arizona, but from an old trapper named Arizona George who trapped the area in the late 1800s.

Q. What former roadway was turned into a sec-

tion of hiking trail near the Jackson Lake Lodge?
A. The old highway to Yellowstone, which ran through willow flats along the base of the hill that the lodge sits on.

Q. How did Schwabacher's Landing get its name?
A. It was named after Albert Schwabacher, a wealthy investor from San Francisco who owned a ranch along the Snake River there. Albert bought numerous properties in the valley, including the land that is now the Lost Creek Ranch and the old George Ferrel homestead that is now known as Schwabacher's.

HISTORY

GRAND TETON NATIONAL PARK

Q. Who is credited with the very first idea of creating a national park to protect the Tetons?
A. Charles D. Walcott, head of the U.S. Geological Survey, in 1898.

Q. What term did he use to describe the Tetons?
A. The "Switzerland of America."

Q. When was Grand Teton National Park formed?
A. 1929.

Q. How many years did it take to turn Grand Teton National Park from an idea into a reality?
A. Fifty-two years.

Q. Why did Congress feel it necessary to begin a program of artificial feeding for the elk in Jackson Hole in the early 1900s?
A. Each winter, elk from Yellowstone National Park migrated to lower elevations to find food and avoid severe weather. Large herds of elk spent their winters at Jackson Hole. However, with the rising number of ranchers in the area, accompanied by fences and cattle, the amount of food available to elk became limited. They began to starve by the thousands.

Q. How did the situation with the elk play a role in the formation of Grand Teton National Park?
A. Charles D. Walcott, director of the United States Geological Survey, thought it incongruous for the government to protect the elk in their summer range in Yellowstone National Park but not in their winter range in Jackson Hole. He suggested either incorporating the Tetons and Jackson Hole into Yellowstone, or creating a separate park.

Q. What president established the Teton Forest Reserve, which included most of the land that makes up Grand Teton National Park today?
A. Grover Cleveland, in 1897.

Q. What President recommended the establishment of a Bureau of National Parks?
A. William Howard Taft.

Q. What happened to his recommendation four years later, in 1916?
A. It became law through the National Park Service Act.

Q. Who were the two men put in charge of the national parks in 1917?
A. Stephen Mather, a millionaire industrialist and conservationist, was appointed the first director of the National Park Service. Horace M. Albright was his young aide.

Q. When did these two men first see the Tetons and decide to preserve the area?
A. In 1916, while Mather was promoting the pending national park legislation in Yellowstone, he and Albright took a side trip to the Tetons.

Q. In the early 1920s the land that would become Grand Teton National Park was administered by the U.S. Forest Service. How did the National Park Service manage to keep control of the land until it could be set aside as a park?
A. An Executive Order by President Woodrow Wilson effectively gave the National Park Service veto power over any actions proposed near the Tetons.

Q. Using this power, what two major projects did the National Park Service veto?
A. A plan to dam Jenny Lake and a plan to dam Emma Matilda and Two Ocean lakes.

Q. How large was the park in 1929?
A. Only 96,000 acres, just the land west of the Teton Park Road—basically the lakes and the Tetons. That's less than one-third the current size of the park.

Q. How many people staffed Grand Teton National Park the first year?
A. Five, and two of them were seasonal. Today, the park employs about 130 people year round and up to 200 during the summer.

Q. What was the 1929 budget for the park?
A. $11,750. That would be about $400,000 in today's money. Today's budgets are in the range of $20-$30 million.

Q. What was the first brand new trail built in the park?
A. The Jenny Lake Trail that circles Jenny Lake, in 1930.

Q. What was the first trail improved and constructed into the Tetons by trail crews of the new park in 1930?
A. The trail to Amphitheater Lake and Teton Glacier.

Q. What was the first improved trail into the Tetons, including the years before the area became a national park?
A. In 1921 the Death Canyon Trail was improved into a serviceable trail by the U.S. Forest Service. Before that it was used occasionally by prospectors as a late summer route to Idaho (the remains of a prospector's cabin and diggings remain today at the head of the canyon) and by stockmen to access their sheep and cattle in the high country. One version of the origin of the name "Death Canyon" is that a sheepherder was killed there by cattlemen in a dispute over grazing rights during the "range wars" at the turn of the 20th century.

Q. By 1931, how many miles of trails had been built in the park?
A. 60.

Q. How many miles of hiking trails are there today?
A. Nearly 200.

Q. How many miles of paved roads are in the park?
A. About 100.

Q. What is a concessionaire?
A. A person or company licensed to operate a commercial business in a national park.

Q. What were the first concessionaire businesses in the park?
A. Pack horses, fishing boats on Jenny Lake, and an inn, all in 1930.

Q. What national event occurred just after the park opened?
A. The Great Depression.

Q. What Depression-fighting effort of President Franklin Roosevelt sent workers to Grand Teton?
A. The Civilian Conservation Corps (CCC), part of Roosevelt's New Deal program.

Q. What was their most significant task?
A. They cleaned up all the dead trees along the shores of Jackson Lake. The trees had been killed when a new dam raised the lake's water level, flooding the pine forest.

Q. How many acres of trees were flooded?
A. 7,000.

Q. What government agency had jurisdiction over the Tetons before the park was formed?
A. The peaks were included in Teton National Forest, created in 1908 by Executive Order of President Theodore Roosevelt.

Q. What millionaire philanthropist visited the Teton National Forest in 1924, 1926, and 1931, inspiring him to get involved in the valley's protection for the rest of his life?
A. John D. Rockefeller, Jr.

Q. What did he do?
A. He agreed to fund the purchase of private land within and around the fledgling Grand Teton National Park in order to protect it from commercialization.

Q. Attracting a wealthy philanthropist to buy up the land was the dream of a group of local men and women. What did they call their vision for preserving the Tetons and Jackson Hole?
A. The Jackson Hole Plan. It was conceived by a mix of ranchers, bureaucrats, and dude ranchers at a meeting in 1923 in a little log cabin in the town of Moose. Their plan continued even after Grand Teton National Park was formed in 1929.

Q. What was the colorful expression they used to describe their goal for all of Jackson Hole?
A. A "museum on the hoof." In other words, they wanted Jackson Hole to retain its Western character, scenery, and wildlife,

and not be developed. They were actually opposed to making the Tetons a national park.

Q. Where was the log cabin where this meeting was held?
A. The cabin was the home of Maude Noble, the woman who purchased Menor's Ferry in 1918. Her cabin still stands at Moose and is open to the public.

Q. What is an inholding?
A. A piece of private property surrounded by public lands.

Q. What inholdings prompted Rockefeller to get involved in the preservation of Grand Teton National Park?
A. A string of dilapidated rental cabins, a dance hall, a gas station, and a bar stretched along the road right in front of the Tetons. Rockefeller was dismayed at the scene and decided to fund the effort to purchase and remove the clutter that detracted from the beautiful Teton scenery.

Q. What was the name of the company Rockefeller started in order to buy ranch land and park inholdings?
A. The Snake River Land Company, formed in 1927.

Q. What did Rockefeller do after Grand Teton National Park was established in 1929?
A. He kept on buying land around the park—in secret.

Q. Why was secrecy needed?
A. Rockefeller intended to turn over his land to the government for an expanded Grand Teton National Park, and many of the local residents were fiercely opposed to the federal government owning more land. Rockefeller also thought that if it became known he was behind the buying, land prices might become inflated.

Q. When was Rockefeller's ruse uncovered?
A. In 1930, when suspicious news reporters got too close to the truth, Rockefeller's involvement was revealed to the public.

Q. What was the public reaction?
A. There were local protests against Rockefeller's plan and a newspaper dedicated to undoing the land preservation was launched. There was even a sub-committee hearing held in the U.S. Senate. Although opposition to Rockefeller's efforts was loud, most of the ranchers and homesteaders who had sold to his company had done so willingly and at a more-than-fair prices.

Q. How much land had Rockefeller's Snake River Land Company purchased by then?
A. More than 30,000 acres.

Q. What happened next?
A. After some persuasion, President Franklin Roosevelt created the Jackson Hole National Monument in 1943.

Q. How big was the Jackson Hole National Monument?
A. It comprised 221,000 acres of federal land around the existing Grand Teton National Park. Much of this land was on the east side of the Snake River.

Q. What Hollywood movie star got involved in this land controversy?
A. Wallace Beery joined an armed protest that rode horses across former grazing land that was now protected by the new Jackson Hole National Monument. Beery had starred in several westerns filmed in Jackson Hole, including *Wyoming* and *Bad Bascomb,* and had built a home on the shores of Jackson Lake. Beery, of course, sided with the cowboys in their fight against "the big, bad government." His presence brought national attention to the protests.

Q. Cliff Hansen, a local rancher involved in the 1943 protest, was also a county

commissioner. Why did he oppose Rockefeller and Roosevelt?
A. Hansen feared the county would lose much of its tax revenues if the Rockefeller land became government property. He and other ranchers also feared they would lose their grazing rights on any public lands that would be included in a new and larger Grand Teton National Park.

Q. What public offices did Hansen hold later in his life?
A. Hansen went on to become a Wyoming governor and then U.S. Senator.

Q. Did Hansen ever change his mind about the land protest?
A. Hansen later admitted he was glad they had lost the fight, because if they had won, the Tetons would be overwhelmed by commercial development.

Q. How was all the controversy resolved?
A. Eventually the protests and fighting died down, and on September 14, 1950, a new Grand Teton National Park was created by combining the old park of 1929 with the Jackson Hole National Monument.

Q. What happened to all of Rockefeller's land?
A. When he saw that the issue was finally going to be resolved by creating a new park, he donated his land to the United States Government just before the new, enlarged park was formed.

Q. How many acres did Rockefeller donate?
A. 32,117—an area of land more than twice the size of New York's Manhattan Island. Rockefeller's land, which comprised dozens of ranches and small homesteads scattered all over the northern end of the valley, is now included in Grand Teton National Park.

Q. How many acres did he keep for himself?
A. He kept the 1,106-acre JY Ranch, a dude ranch on the shores of Phelps Lake.

Q. Do the Rockefellers still own it?

A. No, in 2007 the JY Ranch was donated to the National Park Service by John D. Rockefeller's son, Laurance S. Rockefeller. It is now known as the Laurance S. Rockefeller Preserve.

Q. What was the value of the ranch when it was donated to the park?

A. $160 million.

Q. How large is the present-day Grand Teton National Park?

A. 310,000 acres.

Q. Why are cattle grazing in Grand Teton National Park?

A. When the park was expanded in 1950 to include the ranchland purchased by John D. Rockefeller, Jr. and donated to the park, 31 ranchers were given leases to continue grazing 4,400 animals on 69,000 acres. These leases were either for the lifetime of the ranchers or their heirs' lifetimes. By 2003, there were 1,780 animals permitted to graze on 28,071 acres.

Q. How did there come to be an airport inside Grand Teton National Park?

A. Although Jackson had a small runway in the 1930s, a larger airport was needed to attract commercial flights. In 1940 the town applied for a permit from both the Interior Department and the Snake River Land Company. Controversy over the best location for an airport delayed the project for a few years. According to local lore, a group of men finally commandeered heavy equipment belonging to the county and scraped out a runway at the airport's present location. A lease for this site was eventually secured, and in 1946 commercial air service was launched. Today the airport operates under a lease from the National Park Service.

Q. Do any other national parks contain a large commercial airport?
A. No, although a number of parks have small runways for official use.

Q. Who was the park's first resident photographer?
A. Harrison Crandall, an artist who took up photography in the 1920s in order to make a living in Jackson Hole.

Q. Where was his studio?
A. On his 120-acre homestead near Jenny Lake. In order to comply with the homestead laws, Crandall grazed 40 horses during the summers and planted brome grass for feed.

Q. What is his studio used for today?
A. The Jenny Lake Visitor Center. Crandall sold his homestead to Rockefeller's Snake River Land Company in 1929 and then persuaded the National Park Service to give him one of the first permits for a commercial business inside the park. He moved his studio to the shores of Jenny Lake and operated it there until 1959, when he retired and gave the log studio to the park.

Q. What other business did Crandall operate?
A. Saturday night dances at his log and canvas dance pavilion.

Q. Who played for the dances?
A. Crandall played the trombone and his wife, Hildegarde, played the piano.

Q. What soon-to-be-famous mountaineer played saxophone and sang in Crandall's dance band?
A. Glenn Exum, who founded the Exum Mountaineering School and guide service, which still operates in the park today.

Q. What famous photographer returned to Jackson Hole in the 1930s and had his photo taken by Harrison Crandall?
A. William H. Jackson, first person to photograph the Tetons.

Q. When did the first automobile venture into Jackson Hole?
A. In 1908 a car crossed over Togwotee Pass from Fort Washakie and went as far as the South Entrance to Yellowstone.

Q. What was particularly ironic about the passengers of this first automobile?
A. They were tourists.

Q. A mother and son developed their small homestead in Moose into tourist facilities that still operate today. What was their family name?
A. Dornan. The business, Moose Enterprises, includes a chuck-wagon restaurant, a bar and store, and guest cabins. Homesteaded in 1922 by Evelyn Dornan, the land sits in the middle of Grand Teton National Park. The business was started by Evelyn's son John P. Dornan, and he built it into a tourist destination as well as a world-class wine shop.

Q. Present-day Jackson is visited by thousands of cars every day. How many cars per day drove through Jackson in 1915?
A. 5 to 15 cars per day.

Q. What landmark number did park visitation reach in 1992?
A. Three million visitors for the year.

Q. When was the Chapel of the Sacred Heart, a log church near Signal Mountain Lodge, built?
A. 1937. It was built for the small population in the Moran area.

Q. Cunningham Cabin, a historic site in Grand Teton National Park, was named for what person?
A. Rancher and homesteader John Pierce Cunningham, who arrived in the valley from New York in 1885.

Q. What violent event took place at Cunningham's cabin in the spring of 1893?

A. A posse surrounded a cabin where two alleged horse thieves were holed up for the winter and shot the men to death when they emerged from the building. Cunning-ham had given the men permission to winter their horses on his property, but he and oth-er valley ranchers became suspicious. In the spring, two men from Montana arrived and identified themselves as lawmen. They orga-nized the posse. The alleged horse thieves, named Spenser and Burnett, were buried at the cabin and the posse dispersed.

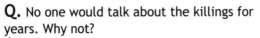

Q. No one would talk about the killings for years. Why not?
A. It appears the two "lawmen" may have been guns-for-hire sent to even a score, and they duped the local men into joining their murderous plan.

Q. What occupied the spot of the present-day Blacktail Ponds Overlook, just north of Moose?
A. The homestead of Henry Gunther, who claimed it in 1914. Gunther had a house and barn and extensive hay fields. Rem-nants of the buildings' foundations can still be found in the sagebrush near the overlook parking lot.

Q. At the place where the road to Lupine Meadows crosses Cottonwood Creek, there is an area of park employee housing. What was this place before it belonged to the park?
A. It began in 1914 as the homestead of a man named Harry Sensenbach. Unable to make a living as a farmer on the poor soil, he and his wife turned their home into a restaurant and built rental cabins. Reportedly, they also sold a little bootleg whiskey and beer during the Prohibition. After Prohibition end-ed they continued to run their home as a popular beer parlor and restaurant. After changing hands a couple times, it became the property of Byron Jenkins, who enlarged the facility and named it the Highlands Lodge. In 1972 he sold it to the National Park Service.

Q. On the east edge of Lupine Meadows, across the creek from the old Highlands Lodge, there is a cluster of cabins used seasonally by the park as employee housing and as a base for the Jenny Lake Rescue Rangers. What were these cabins originally?
A. They were part of a commercial enterprise in the 1930s owned by a man named J.D. Kimmel. He built rental cabins along Cottonwood Creek and a two-story building on the east side of the creek. For years this building housed the Jenny Lake Post Office. Kimmel sold to the park in 1944, and the store and post office were removed in 1962.

Q. What personal habit was Kimmel known for locally?
A. He always wore a Colt .45 pistol on his right hip. Kimmel had been in the oil business in Oklahoma, and the rumor was that he had been involved with some shady characters who might track him to Wyoming.

Q. There is a series of deep depressions in the ground along highway 89/191 as it winds its way up the Jackson Hole valley in front of the Tetons. Each depression is about the size of a football field and roughly fifteen to twenty feet deep. There is one near the north end of Blacktail Butte and one across the highway from the airport that is used for vehicle storage by the National Park Service. Are these depressions natural or man-made?
A. They are man-made. When the highway was built between 1955 and 1957, rock and gravel for the roadway was taken from these borrow pits rather than trucked in from outside the park. Although they are called "borrow" pits, it's highly unlikely the material will ever be returned.

Q. Along highway 89/191 a mile-and-a half south of Moose Junction, there is an odd, out-of-place bump in the otherwise level sagebrush flats. It's on the west (mountain) side of the highway, about a hundred yards off the road and just two tenths of a mile north of the Meadow Road turnoff. What is this strange little knob made of?
A. Horse bones. In the 1940s the area was cultivated ranch land, and one day the ranch horses got into a barrel of poi-

soned oats intended for killing gophers in the alfalfa fields. There were too many dead horses to bury properly, so one of the ranch hands, a rodeo cowboy named Ted Hartgrave, used a tractor to pile the carcasses in a large heap and cover them with dirt and rocks.

AMERICAN INDIANS

Q. When did the first humans arrive in what is now Grand Teton National Park?
A. About 12,000 years ago.

Q. What were the first inhabitants called?
A. Paleoindians, meaning "ancient Indians" or prehistoric Native Americans.

Q. How old is the oldest evidence found so far of humans in Jackson Hole?
A. A stone spear point 11,000 years old.

Q. What else did the Paleoindians leave behind?

A. Among other things, archaeologists have found an 8,000-year-old obsidian knife, a few spear points, and campsites.

Q. Did the early Paleoindians live here all year?
A. No, the Paleoindians just visited seasonally for food and obsidian.

Q. What is obsidian?
A. Obsidian is a rock, also known as volcanic glass, that can shaped into arrowheads, spear points, and cutting tools. Paleoindians gathered obsidian from Teton Pass, Obsidian Cliff, and sites in the Targhee National Forest.

Q. What property of obsidian helps archaeologists study prehistoric Indians?

A. Each volcanic flow of obsidian has unique properties that can be identified like fingerprints. This enables archaeologists to trace the source of obsidian artifacts found many miles from the original quarry.

Q. How far from the Teton/Yellowstone quarries have obsidian artifacts from those quarries been found?
A. Traded from tribe to tribe, they reached southern Ohio.

Q. What makes obsidian ideal for arrowheads, spear points, and knives?
A. It flakes well (allowing it to be crafted into a desired shape) and it holds a razor-sharp edge.

Q. What is obsidian used for today?
A. It is made into surgical scalpels that are sharper than steel. They are used in cardiac and cosmetic surgery where an extremely fine incision is needed.

Q. Did the Paleoindians live in tipis?
A. No—we are not sure what they lived in. The tipi was developed later.

Q. During a time from 7,000 years ago to 1,500 years ago, how did the Paleoindians who came to the Tetons cook their food?
A. They dug roasting pits that they lined with rocks. A fire was built in the pit until the rocks got hot, then the coals were scooped out and edible plants were put into the pit and covered up. The roasting pits worked like ovens.

Q. Where have these roasting pits been found in Jackson Hole?
A. In the northern end of the park, where food plants were most abundant.

Q. What weapon did the Paleoindians hunt with before the bow and arrow, in the period from 3,000 to 1,500 years before present?
A. The atlatl, a type of throwing device made of a stick fitted with a thong or socket to steady the butt of a spear or dart and extend the length of the throw.

Q. When did the bow and arrow come into use?
A. Beginning about 1,500 years ago, the bow gradually replaced the atlatl.

Q. When did American Indians first acquire horses?
A. About AD 1700.

Q. Were these horses native to North America?
A. No, they were brought here about AD 1500 by Europeans. Most of the horses used by tribes of this area came from herds stolen from or abandoned by Spanish explorers and settlers in the southwestern U.S.

Q. How did the Indians haul their belongings before they had horses?
A. They used large dogs as pack animals.

Q. What device did the Indians use with their pack dogs, and later with horses, to haul their belongings?
A. The travois, a V-shaped arrangement of two poles attached to the animal and dragging on the ground be-
hind. A framework between the poles created a place to carry tipi hides, food, and even sick or elderly members of the tribe.

Q. The tipi covers used by various tribes of the Great Plains were made of buffalo hides that had been tanned. How much did a tipi cover weigh?
A. Buffalo-hide tipi covers collected by Spanish explorers in 1599 weighed about fifty pounds.

Q. How much does a comparable modern-day canvas wall tent weigh?
A. About 80 pounds, or 30 pounds more than a tipi of similar size.

Q. Besides the hide, what other buffalo part was used in the tanning process?
A. The brain, which was rubbed into the hide to make it soft. Once the hide was scraped clean of all hair and flesh it was hung over a smoldering fire to be smoked and dried, then a paste of cooked brains was smeared on both sides of the hide and allowed to soak in. Oils and other compounds in the brains replaced the lost moisture in the hide, and after the hide was "worked"—rubbed and stretched—it turned soft and virtually waterproof.

Q. What tree was preferred for making tipi poles?
A. The lodgepole pine, hence its name. The lodgepole pine grows tall with a slender trunk.

Q. Who were the first modern Indians to live in Jackson Hole?
A. None actually lived here year round, but the valley was a fairly common seasonal destination for migrating tribes. Shoshone and their ancestors have been here continuously, but seasonally, for at least 11,000 years.

Q. Did the Paleoindians leave when the modern tribes arrived?
A. No. The constantly migrating Paleoindians gradually learned new skills and customs to evolve into the modern tribes we know today.

Q. What cultural change generally marks the beginning of modern tribes?

A. The appearance of European influences such as tools, trade goods, and horses. There was not much cultural change in American Indians from 11,000 years ago to about 500 years ago. The arrival of Europeans changed everything.

Q. The Shoshone, the modern Indians that inhabited this region (and still do), consisted of many local tribes that lived over a broad area from the Cascade Mountains in the Pacific Northwest to the Northern Plains to the southwest U.S. What characteristic was used to identify the various tribes of Shoshone?
A. They were essentially divided by their ecological niche, or diet. Eastern Shoshone, the Indians who most often came into Jackson Hole, included the *Kucundicka* or Buffalo Eaters, and the *Pa'lahiadika* or Elk Eaters.

Q. The Mountain Shoshones, also known as the Sheep Eaters or the *Tukadika*, lived in the mountainous region surrounding Jackson Hole—the Tetons, Yellowstone, the Absarokas, and the Wind River Range. What remnants of their lifestyle still remain in Jackson Hole?
A. Sheep traps, which were fences and barriers made of log

and stone designed to funnel Rocky Mountain bighorn sheep into a camouflaged pen where they could be killed.

Q. Did the Shoshone stick together all year?
A. No, tribes would split into bands in winter and spring, into family groups in summer, and reunite in the fall for traditional hunts.

Q. Why did the Shoshone come to Jackson Hole?
A. For food, and for spiritual ties to the landscape and the mountains.

Q. Togwotee Pass, just east of Grand Teton National Park, was named for a Sheep Eater medicine man named Togwotee. After being relocated to the Wind River Indian Reservation, Togwotee became a guide for expeditions through the mountains of Yellowstone and Grand Teton. Who was the most famous person he guided?
A. U.S. President Chester Arthur, in 1883. Togwotee's descendents still live on the Wind River Reservation.

Q. What other Indian tribes came here?
A. The Tetons were a navigation landmark, and other tribes such as the Nez Perce, Bannock, Crow, Blackfeet, and Gros Ventre passed through the Jackson Hole valley on their way to trade, hunt, or war in other places.

Q. What disease killed 66 percent of the Blackfeet Indians by 1870?
A. Smallpox, a viral disease that dates back to at least Egyptian times. Smallpox epidemics in the 1700s and 1800s killed many American colonists as well as Native Americans. Both George Washington and Abraham Lincoln contracted the deadly disease and survived.

Q. When did the Shoshone quit coming here?
A. They haven't. Modern-day Shoshone Indians still visit or work here each year.

Q. Who was the most famous Shoshone?
A. Sacajawea, the young Eastern Shoshone woman who led Lewis and Clark through the Rocky Mountains to the Pacific Ocean.

Q. What well-known Shoshone war chief has numerous landmarks in Wyoming named after him?
A. Chief Washakie has a U.S. Army fort (now a town), a mountain, a county, a lake, and a national forest named in his

honor. He was considered the head of the Eastern Shoshones by the representatives of the United States government. Upon his death in 1900, he became the only known Native American to be given a full military funeral.

Q. What 12-year-old white settler boy ran away to live with Chief Washakie and the Shoshone tribe for two years?
A. Nick Wilson, who later founded the town of Wilson at the foot of the Tetons just west of Jackson.

Q. What book chronicles Nick's story?
A. *The White Indian Boy: The Story of Uncle Nick Among the Shoshones* by Elijah Nicholas Wilson.

Q. In the 1920s a white couple began their life-long study of the American Plains Indians. They lived in Jackson Hole from the 1940s until their deaths in the late 1990s and had their home in Moose, inside Grand Teton National Park. Who were they?
A. Reginald and Gladys Laubin. Their best-selling book, *The Indian Tipi* (1957), became the tipi bible for everyone from historians to hippies.

Q. Who was the Sioux Indian that adopted the Laubins in the 1930s?
A. Chief One Bull, nephew of Sitting Bull.

EXPLORERS, TRADERS, AND TRAPPERS

Q. Who was the first European (white man) to see Jackson Hole?
A. John Colter, who originally came out west with Lewis and Clark, was long credited with the feat. However, most scholars today believe he didn't actually reach the valley in his wanderings during the winter of 1807, as is claimed.

Q. What attribute of Colter's do his supporters point to when

arguing that he could have easily made the grueling trip into the valley in winter?
A. His strength and endurance, highlighted by his famous escape from the Blackfeet Indians.

Q. How far did Colter have to travel to escape the Blackfeet?
A. He ran for five miles and then hid in a beaver pond until his pursuers left. After that, he walked 300 miles to the nearest trading post.

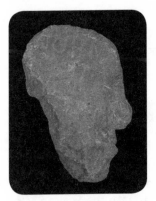

Q. What artifact came to light in 1933 to confuse the issue of Colter's visit?
A. The Colter Stone, a rock carved into the shape of a human head with the inscription, "John Colter 1808." It was plowed up just west of the Tetons in 1931.

Q. What do experts believe to be the origin of this stone?
A. Most think it's either a hoax or possibly a stone carved by a member of the 1872 Hayden Expedition to the Tetons.

Q. What fact appears to support the authenticity of the Colter Stone?
A. For many years historians dated Colter's alleged visit to Jackson Hole as occurring in 1807, relying on the date of Lewis and Clark's maps, but more recent research puts him here in the winter of 1808, the date on the stone, and only Colter would have known that. Also, it was a fairly common practice to carve names and dates in stone at a time when there was no other material for marking one's presence in a new land.

Q. What did Colter say about his trip to the Tetons?
A. He didn't. Colter himself never claimed to have "discovered" the valley and its mountains.

Q. If not John Colter, who were the first white men to the area?
A. Fur trappers working for the Missouri Fur Company trapped here in 1810-1811, but their names are not known.

Q. Who were the first men we can name?
A. Trappers John Hoback, Edward Robinson, and Jacob Reznor. These men had been employed at Henry's Fort on the Henry's Fork of the Snake River, but they gave up trapping and headed back east. In 1811 they crossed Teton Pass, went through Jackson Hole, and left via Togwotee Pass.

Q. Did these men ever return?
A. Yes, they actually turned around and came right back as guides.

Q. What group did these men guide through Jackson Hole?
A. The Overland Astorians, a group of trappers formed by John Jacob Astor and bound for Oregon to set up a trading post. When fur trappers Hoback, Reznor, and Robinson reached the Missouri River, they met the Astorians and agreed to guide them back through the Rockies. They traveled down the Hoback River (named later for John Hoback) until it ran into the Snake River and then followed it upstream to Jackson Hole. They left via Teton Pass.

Q. What was the Snake River known as then?
A. The Mad River.

Q. What were the mountain men called during their own time—the early 1800s?
A. Mountaineers.

Q. What did the mountain men/fur trappers find to trap in Jackson Hole?
A. Beaver.

Q. Why were beaver hides so valuable?
A. The fur was used in Europe for men's hats—the height of fashion in the early 1800s.

Q. What made beaver fur so good for hats?
A. To make a felt hat, beaver fur was cut from the hide, mixed

with other fur, and pressed into felt. Beaver fur was important because the under-fur of beaver has tiny barbs for trapping air bubbles and insulating the beaver in cold water. These barbs made the other fur in the felt stick tightly together, forming the best and longest lasting felt available.

Q. How much were beaver hides worth?
A. $6 a pound. That would be nearly $200 per pound in today's money. Depending on the size of the beaver, one dried hide weighed about 2 to 3 pounds.

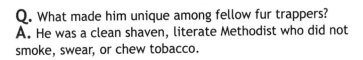

Q. What famous mountain man trapped here in the early 1800s?
A. Jedediah Smith.

Q. What made him unique among fellow fur trappers?
A. He was a clean shaven, literate Methodist who did not smoke, swear, or chew tobacco.

Q. Why did he wear his hair long?
A. To cover his missing ear, ripped off by a grizzly bear.

Q. What nearby area bears his name?
A. The Jedediah Smith Wilderness, on the west edge of the Tetons.

Q. What fur trapper was the valley of Jackson Hole named for?
A. David E. Jackson. Originally it was called Jackson's Hole, but the apostrophe and the "s" were later dropped.

Q. What does the word "hole" in Jackson Hole mean?
A. A "hole" was the fur trappers' term for a mountain valley. Just west of the Tetons lies Pierre's Hole.

Q. Who named Jackson's Hole for Jackson?
A. Supposedly his business partner, William Sublette, started calling it Jackson's Hole in 1829.

Q. What fur trapper and partner to Sublette was known by the Indian name, Broken Hand?
A. Tom Fitzpatrick, who had a rifle explode in his hands.

Q. What event led to Fitzpatrick's nickname being changed to White Hair?
A. While being chased by Gros Ventre Indians, he lost his horse and had to escape on foot. He hid in rocks and under brush for two days while the Indians scoured the area for him, at one point almost stepping on him. When the Indians gave up, Fitzpatrick went on but lost his rifle, was attacked by wolves, and finally was rescued while attempting to ford the Snake River. After this ordeal his hair grew out white.

Q. What other famous mountain man traveled through Jackson Hole and now has dozens of places named after him?
A. Jim Bridger.

Q. Who was Jim Bridger's third wife?
A. Mary Washakie, daughter of the great Shoshone, Chief Washakie.

Q. What educated mountain man kept detailed journals of his days as a fur trapper in Jackson's Hole?
A. Osborne Russell, whose meticulous records of his experiences from 1834 to 1843 gives us a glimpse into the everyday life of a mountain man.

Q. What event caused Osborne Russell to have a miserable 4th of July in Jackson Hole in 1835?
A. His bullskin boat capsized while he and some other trappers were trying to cross the Snake River. They made it to shore but

spent a rough night trying to stay warm and figure out how to survive without all their gear and weapons. Fortunately, they found their boat downstream.

Q. What was different about mountain man Jim Beckwourth?
A. He was black—the son of a Virginia aristocrat and a black slave woman.

Q. What extraordinary feat did Beckwourth accomplish?
A. He became a War Chief of the Crow tribe. According to the legend, a fellow trapper made up a tale about Beckwourth's ancestry and passed it along to the Crows at a rendezvous. Later, while on a hunting trip with Jim Bridger, Beckwourth was captured by the Crows and identified as Big Bowl, the long-lost son of a Crow chief. Beckwourth spent a number of years living with the Crow Indians.

Q. Among his peers, what was Beckwourth famous for?
A. Exaggerating the facts.

Q. Despite embellishing his stories a great deal, Beckwourth had the fortune (or misfortune) of showing up just in time for historic events. For example, he arrived in California just in time for the start of the Gold Rush of 1849, but on his way there he stumbled upon the gruesome murder of 11 people at the San Miguel Mission, an infamous crime in California history. What did Beckwourth do?
A. Beckwourth joined the posse that tracked down the murderers near Santa Barbara. One of the men turned state's evidence, but, as Beckwourth said later, "We shot them, including the state's evidence."

Q. Why and when did the era of the mountain man end?
A. About 1840 the wearing of beaver fur hats went out of style. This change in fashion virtually ended the demand for beaver hides.

Q. What was a mountain man *rendezvous*?
A. This was a huge annual event lasting a week or more in the

summer, where trappers brought their winter's catch of furs and met supply wagons from St. Louis. At its peak, the rendezvous might include five hundred or more trappers, a thousand Indians, and thousands of horses. The first rendezvous was held in 1825. The last rendezvous was held near the Green River in 1840, signifying the end of an era.

Q. What gruesome event occurred at the 1833 Rendezvous near present-day Daniel, Wyoming, just 60 miles southeast of Jackson Hole?
A. A rabid wolf bit twelve drunken mountain men while they were celebrating. Most of the twelve men contracted rabies and died. One man began to howl and foam at the mouth—he had the presence of mind to warn off his friends and disappeared into the wilderness to die.

Q. What was John Jacob Astor, founder of the American Fur Company and provider of trade goods to the mountain man rendezvous, eventually known for?
A. He was the first multi-millionaire in the U.S. and the richest man in the world.

Q. Who comprised the next wave of visitors to the Tetons and Jackson Hole?
A. U.S. government surveyors, engineers, and scientists sent to evaluate potential routes to the Pacific coast. They also assessed the territory for minerals and other natural resources.

Q. Who led the first survey party into Jackson Hole?
A. Captain W.F. Raynolds, in 1860.

Q. Who was his guide?
A. Legendary explorer and mountain man Jim Bridger.

Q. What feat did Jim Bridger manage to pull off on this trip?

A. He got them lost. Bridger was known for his incredible path-finding skills, but the 56-year-old mountain man was apparently beginning to lose his famed memory for details of the landscape. After floundering for a few days in the upper Gros Ventre country, he followed the Gros Ventre River into Jackson Hole and regained his bearings.

Q. During Walter DeLacy's 1863 expedition to prospect for gold in Jackson Hole, did he find any?
A. He found no gold worth the effort to recover it, but more significant was the lack of any human sign—either white or Indian. Despite his negative report, prospectors worked the streams of Jackson Hole for years trying to find the source for the traces of gold that enticed them. When Uncle Jack Davis, a local prospector, died after 20 years of working his claim, he only had about $12 worth of gold.

Q. What characterized the 1876 survey led by Lieutenant Gustavus Cheney Doane?
A. It was a disaster, with Doane losing wagons, horses, equipment, food, and mules all along the way. At one point Doane and his men were forced to eat a river otter, and they later killed and ate one of their horses. By the time they returned to civilization, Doane had lost more than 60 pounds.

Q. What major scientific survey explored the Tetons in 1872?
A. The Snake River Division of the Hayden Surveys. Ferdinand V. Hayden mapped Yellowstone, while his Snake River Division mapped the Tetons.

Q. Hayden was the premier explorer of his day, organizing many expeditions to explore and map the West. What was his field of study?
A. He was a surgeon.

Q. What two "firsts" happened in the Teton area during the 1872 Hayden expedition?
A. The first photographs were taken of the Tetons (from the west side), by William H. Jackson, and the Grand Teton was

first climbed (reportedly, anyway) by survey leader James Stevenson and his guest Nathaniel P. Langford, the superintendent of Yellowstone National Park.

Q. What did James Stevenson try to rename the Grand Teton?
A. He called it Mount Hayden, after his boss Ferdinand Hayden, but the name change didn't take.

Q. Artist Thomas Moran sketched and painted the Tetons for the first time in 1879, and Mount Moran and the town of Moran on the east side of the Tetons are named for him. What is ironic about this?

A. He never actually visited Jackson Hole, but painted the mountains from the west side.

Q. Where does one of Thomas Moran's paintings of the Tetons now hang?
A. In the White House.

Q. What local mountain man guided the Hayden survey through Jackson Hole?
A. Richard "Beaver Dick" Leigh, a red-bearded expatriate Brit.

Q. What two lakes in Grand Teton National Park were named for Beaver Dick Leigh and his Indian wife, Jenny Leigh?
A. Leigh Lake and Jenny Lake.

Q. What documents did Beaver Dick Leigh leave to posterity?
A. His poignant journal and letters about his wife and children dying of smallpox. In the winter of 1876, the Leigh family sheltered a woman whose family had died of smallpox. As a result, the entire Leigh family contracted the disease. Jenny and the five children died; Dick became ill but survived.

Q. What two popular lakes in Grand Teton National Park are named after other members of the 1872 survey?

A. Bradley and Taggart lakes are named after geologist Frank Bradley and his assistant William Taggart.

Q. Who took the first photographs of the Tetons from the east side, as they are viewed in Grand Teton National Park?
A. William H. Jackson, on a return trip to the valley in 1878.

Q. How did W.H. Jackson describe the valley he photographed for the first time?
A. "...the beautiful valley that has the distressing name of Jackson's Hole."

Q. At the time, Jackson was so thin that he needed what in order to travel by horseback?
A. He required a pillow on his saddle.

Q. What well-known American visited Jackson's Hole in 1883, even before there were any permanent residents living here?
A. President Chester A. Arthur came through on a fishing and sightseeing trip. Arthur traveled in a huge party of 175 pack animals and 75 cavalrymen but did not allow reporters or women to join the party. It was apparently a men's trip with an emphasis on fishing and drinking.

Q. Where did President Arthur camp on land that is now contained within Grand Teton National Park?
A. Near the Gros Ventre Junction south of Blacktail Butte, and near Moran Junction.

HOMESTEADERS

Q. When did the first homesteaders arrive in Jackson Hole?
A. In 1884 two former fur trappers, John Holland and John Carnes, along with Carnes' wife Millie Sorelle, came to the valley to live.

Q. When did Wyoming become a state?
A. 1890.

Q. What was the population of Jackson Hole in 1890?
A. 64 people.

Q. How many years had nearby Yellowstone been a national park before the first homesteaders arrived in Jackson Hole?
A. 12 years.

Q. Why did it take so long for the valley to be settled?
A. It was isolated, it had long, harsh winters, and there was plenty of better land for homesteading in other places.

Q. In 1885, Robert Miller arrived in Jackson Hole to homestead, bringing the first wagon over Teton Pass. He became a prominent businessman and the valley's first banker. What was his nickname?
A. Old Twelve Percent. Miller was president of the bank and used his position to great effect, charging high-interest loans when he was able to.

Q. What did Miller do for John D. Rockefeller, Jr.?
A. Miller was hired by Rockefeller's organization, the Snake River Land Company, to buy land in Jackson Hole in the 1930s and 1940s. However, Miller was never told what the intention was or who was behind the company.

Q. Why was Miller never told who he was buying land for or why?
A. Because Rockefeller was buying land to expand Grand Teton National Park, and Miller himself was opposed to the idea of expanding the park.

Q. Where was Miller's homestead?
A. On land that is now the National Elk Refuge. His home, the Miller House, still stands and is open to the public.

Q. What law gave Americans and foreigners alike the right to homestead land?
A. The Homestead Act of 1862.

Q. How much did it cost someone to homestead 160 acres?
A. There was a $15 filing fee, and the settler had to live on the land and cultivate it for five years.

Q. How did the homesteader prove they had done the required work?
A. Besides sending in annual reports, the homesteader would be visited by an inspector at the end of the five years.

Q. 160 acres wasn't really enough land for a viable cattle ranch in Jackson Hole. How did ranchers enlarge their property?
A. The Desert Land Act of 1877 allowed them to buy up to 640 additional acres at $1.25 an acre.

Q. In 1892 and 1893 William O. Owen was the first surveyor to set township and section lines in the valley. What historic feat did he accomplish in 1898?
A. He led the first confirmed ascent of the Grand Teton.

Q. What lake in Grand Teton National Park is named for William Owen's wife?
A. Emma Matilda Lake.

Q. Life in Jackson Hole was hard in those days. What was the mortality rate for the valley's children in 1900?
A. 18%. Today it is about 0.07%.

Q. The census of 1900 reported 63 foreign-born settlers in Jackson Hole. From which country did most of them come?
A. Sweden, with 15. England was second with 10, followed by Canada (8); Germany (7); Austria, Denmark, and Scotland (4

each); Switzerland (3); Holland, Norway, and Wales (2 each); and France and Ireland (1 each).

Q. Who was the first homesteader to settle on land that is now in Grand Teton National Park?
A. William Menor. Earlier homesteaders chose prime land toward the southern end of the valley where the soil was better and the winters were slightly milder. Except for a few sites, most of the land destined to become Grand Teton National Park was too rocky and dry for farming.

Q. What did Menor build and operate near Moose in 1894?
A. A river-powered ferry that crossed the Snake River. This type of ferry operates by using the flow of the river to push the ferry across; the ferryboat consists of two large, boat-shaped pontoons with a deck on top. The ferry is attached to a strong cable strung across the river. When the pilot turns the ferry at an angle to the river current, the water slowly pushes the boat across to the other shore.

Q. Why did Menor pick that particular site for his ferry?
A. It's the only spot along the Snake River where the entire stream is in one, deep channel and both river banks are solid. Most of the river meanders back and forth in braided channels that are too shallow and seasonal for a ferry crossing.

Q. How much did Menor charge to cross the Snake River?
A. 50 cents for a wagon and team, and 25 cents for a horse and rider. In today's money, that would be about $30 for the wagon and $15 for the horse and rider.

Q. What else was Bill Menor famous for?
A. His temper, his swearing, and his huckleberry wine.

Q. Who lived directly across the river from Bill Menor?
A. His brother Holiday Menor, who operated a lime kiln.

Q. What was Holiday Menor famous for?
A. He had a worse temper and swore even more than his brother Bill.

Q. How long did the brothers go without speaking to each other after one especially harsh disagreement?
A. Two years.

Q. How long did Bill Menor's ferry operate?
A. He sold it in 1918 to a woman named Maude Noble. She ran it until 1927 when a steel bridge was built just downstream of the ferry. The National Park Service still operates a replica of the ferry when water levels are sufficient to cross the river. This occurs in mid-summer after the spring high water has receded and before the river flow decreases in the fall.

Q. Who was the second homesteader west of the Snake River on land now inside the park?
A. James Manges, who settled along Cottonwood Creek between Jenny Lake and the present-day Taggart Lake parking lot.

Q. What building still stands as a testament to Manges's log building skills?
A. The small, steep-roofed log barn in a meadow just north of the Taggart Lake parking lot.

Q. What dietary oddity was James Manges known for?
A. Eating pickled eggs and rancid butter. Although Manges's chickens laid fresh eggs daily, and his milk cow produced fresh milk and butter, he always pickled the extra eggs and stored the extra butter. Not wanting to throw anything out, he ate the  older, pickled eggs first and tried to use up the butter that was going bad. He never caught up.

Q. What retired schoolteacher lived just south of James Manges?

A. Geraldine Lucas.

Q. Where did Geraldine get her teaching degree?

A. Oberlin College in Ohio. Oberlin was known for producing independent women graduates, and Geraldine certainly fit that model. After teaching in New York City, she retired to Jackson Hole and claimed a homestead at the very foot of the Tetons.

Q. What was Geraldine known for?

A. She was the second woman to climb the Grand Teton, at age 59.

Q. What happened to Geraldine's homestead?

A. Her cabin and outbuildings still stand in the meadow where Geraldine built them, along with a cabin built by Harold Fabian, the man who purchased the homestead from Geraldine's heirs after she died in 1938.

Q. What horrible event did the *New York Times* of July 27, 1895, proclaim happened in Jackson's Hole?

A. That Indians had killed everyone in Jackson's Hole, that they had burned all the homes, and that the governor was sending in troops.

Q. What had actually happened?

A. In a dispute with a few Bannock Indians from Idaho who were hunting elk in violation of Wyoming game laws, a local posse arrested a group of Bannocks, including women and children. In the ensuing confusion, one old Indian man was shot and killed. The rest escaped. The settlers, worried about reprisals, asked the governor to send protection, which he did.

Q. When did the first Mormons homestead on land now inside the park?

A. In 1896 a group found suitable homestead land east of Blacktail Butte. Other Mormons had arrived in the valley in 1889.

Q. What land feature drew the Mormons to the Blacktail Butte area?
A. Deep, rich topsoil.

Q. Why did they leave Utah to come north?
A. A severe drought.

Q. What did the area where they settled become known as?
A. Mormon Row.

Q. What Mormon Row buildings are classic photography subjects for visitors to Grand Teton National Park?
A. The T.A. Moulton barn and the pink John Moulton farmhouse.

Q. Although sheep were despised by cattle ranchers, the farmers on Mormon Row kept a few sheep for wool. What derisive nickname did cattlemen call sheep?
A. Range maggots.

Q. Did Wyoming's deadly range wars between cattle and sheep ranchers erupt in Jackson's Hole?
A. No, because except for the few sheep on Mormon Row, Jackson Hole and the Tetons were exclusively cattle country.

Q. What was the name of the town that formed along Mormon Row?
A. Grovont, the phonetic spelling of Gros Ventre, the Indian tribe. Grovont consisted of a post office that opened in 1899, a church, and a school.

Q. Are any of those three buildings still standing?
A. None of them remain on Mormon Row, but the church was moved to the Teton Village Road and became a bar and pizza joint. It still stands today as the bar portion of the Calico Restaurant.

Q. By 1928 rancher Si Ferrin had the valley's largest cattle operation, the 3,600-acre Elk Ranch. Where was his ranch located?
A. In the large, open meadows just south of Moran Junction in Grand Teton National Park.

Q. When Si Ferrin sold his holdings in 1928-29 to the Snake River Land Company, how much money did he receive?
A. He got just over $114,000 for his 3,600 acres, or about $31 an acre. Today, adjusted for inflation, that sale would have earned Si about $1.5 million. For comparison, recent ranch sales (2000-2008) include $75 million for the 710-acre Four Lazy F Ranch near Jackson, $37 million for the 150-acre Teton Valley Ranch near Kelly, and an asking price of $55 million for the 3,011-acre Little Jennie Ranch south of Jackson.

Q. In 1910 a man named Joe Pfeiffer settled on Antelope Flats. How deep did he hand-dig a well in the rocky soil before giving up?
A. 104 feet. After giving up, he walked the half mile to Ditch Creek for fresh water.

Q. What pioneer of photography gave homesteader Stephen Leek his first camera so he could document life in Jackson Hole?
A. George Eastman, founder of Eastman Kodak. Eastman came here to hunt big game and was guided by Charles Wort, an early outfitter and one-time owner of the present-day Signal Mountain Lodge.

Q. What feat did Leek accomplish with his camera?
A. He photographed elk starving in the winter, leading to the establishment of the National Elk Refuge.

Q. What other "first" was Stephen Leek remembered for?
A. He set up the valley's first sawmill.

Q. What park facility now bears his name?

A. Leek's Marina, a boat marina and restaurant on the site where Stephen Leek owned a small lodge and fishing camp.

Q. What feature gave trapper and poacher "Beaver Tooth" Neil his nickname?
A. His two large, protruding front teeth made of gold. Neil lived in the valley from about 1900 into the 1930s.

Q. What trick did Neil often employ to throw game wardens off his trail?
A. He would wear his snowshoes backwards so they would track him in the wrong direction.

Q. What did Neil do on his way home to Jackson after a poaching trial in Evanston?
A. He poached beaver.

Q. Beavertooth Neil also had legitimate businesses—a store and dance hall. What present-day ranch operates on Neil's old property?
A. The Heart Six Ranch, near Moran.

Q. What did homesteaders use for keeping food cold during the summer months?
A. In the winter they cut blocks of ice from Jenny Lake and Jackson Lake and stored the ice in insulated sheds.

Q. What Jackson Hole cowboy was a champion bull rider from the 1930s to the 1950s?
A. Bob Crisp, who won all the big events of his day from Madison Square Garden to Fort Worth.

Q. What famous outlaw did Crisp claim to have met in Jackson Hole?
A. Butch Cassidy.

Q. Why was this so unusual?
A. At the time, Butch was thought to be dead, supposedly having been killed in South America.

Q. What proof of Butch Cassidy did Bob Crisp have?
A. He had a silver dollar that Butch gave him. Bob was a boy at the time and offered to trade dollars with Butch so he would have the outlaw's money. Bob later had the dollar set into a belt buckle.

Q. Why did Butch Cassidy come to Jackson Hole?
A. He came to visit his old gang member, Bert Charter, who had become a respectable Jackson Hole cowboy.

Q. What Jackson Hole homesteader was the 1926 World Champion middleweight wrestler?
A. Mike Yokel.

Q. When and how did the town of Jackson begin?
A. Jackson was not planned as a town to begin with, but it grew out of a collection of small homestead farms and cabins in the late 1890s. It was named in 1894 and had its streets laid out by a surveyor in 1901. Its first community building, The Clubhouse, was built in 1897 and is still standing on the present-day town square. In 1914, the residents filed for incorporation and the official town of "Jackson" was born.

Q. What is the population of Jackson?
A. In 2009, it was about 10,000 residents. But, since it is a resort town, the actual number of people living in town varies greatly over the seasons. In summer, the population soars with workers to accommodate the 3 million visitors who pass through, and in the "shoulder" seasons of spring and fall the population drops.

Q. What was unusual about the Jackson town government of 1920?
A. All five elected officials were women.

DUDE WRANGLERS AND RANCHERS

Q. Where did the term "dude" come from?
A. Real cowboys gave the name to ranch guests who bought brand new outfits—hat, boots, spurs, chaps—to try to fit in. The exact origin of the word is unknown.

Q. What were female dudes called in the early days?
A. Dudines.

Q. What was the first dude ranch in Grand Teton National Park?
A. The JY Ranch, which eventually belonged to John D. Rockefeller, Jr. The ranch was started by Louis Joy, who simply omitted the middle letter of his last name to come up with his brand. Shortly after Joy began, Struthers Burt bought into the operation. Joy and Burt had a parting of the ways, and in 1912 Burt homesteaded the Bar B C as a dude ranch.

Q. What was the JY Ranch worth when it was sold to the Rockefeller operation in 1932?
A. $49,000.

Q. What was the value of the JY when Laurance S. Rockefeller donated it to the park in 2007?
A. $160 million.

Q. What eastern city was home to a great majority of the dudes and dudines who came to Jackson Hole?
A. Philadelphia.

Q. Why were so many visitors from Philadelphia?
A. Early dude ranchers such as Struthers Burt and Horace Carncross (Bar B C Ranch) happened to know a number wealthy people in the Philadelphia area. Burt had also attended Princeton University, where he had made numerous friends and acquain-

tances from Philadelphia. The well-known author Owen Wister, who stayed at the JY Ranch and then built his own home in Jackson Hole, was from Philadelphia. At the time, it was largely word-of-mouth that promoted the Jackson Hole dude ranches and created the "Philadelphia connection."

Q. Which dude ranch became the center of social life in the park?
A. Struthers Burt's Bar B C. The ranch is located a few miles upstream from Moose, along the Snake River. The ranch closed its doors in 1986, and the dilapidated buildings still stand.

Q. Besides owning the Bar B C, what else did Struthers Burt do?
A. He was a writer. A Princeton graduate, Burt started the dude ranch with physician Horace Carncross, intending to convert it to a cattle ranch once it became profitable. His plan was to raise cattle while he developed a writing career. By 1927, the Bar B C could accommodate up to 50 guests at a fee of $300 per person.

Q. What is the title of Struther's most famous book?
A. *Diary of a Dude Wrangler*, published in 1924. Burt's book was a bestseller of its day and is a valuable collector's book today.

Q. What was the reason Burt gave for choosing dudes over cattle as his livelihood?
A. "They winter better than cows."

Q. To what effort did Burt turn his writing skills in the 1920s?
A. He lobbied for the preservation of Jackson Hole and the formation of Grand Teton National Park. Burt died in 1954 in the St. John's Hospital in Jackson. He was 72 years old.

Q. When did the Bar B C finally close its doors?
A. 1986. Burt and Irving Corse, the two remaining owners after

Carncross's heir was bought out, sold to Rockefeller's Snake River Land Company in 1930 with a lifetime lease to keep running it as a dude ranch. In 1935 Burt sold his interest in the ranch in order to pursue his writing full time. The ranch slowly declined over the years until the last lease-holder, Margaretta Corse, died in 1986. The ranch was abandoned and the land and buildings reverted to the National Park Service.

Q. What did the Elbo Ranch owners build in 1926 on their property along Cottonwood Creek and at the south end of Timbered Island?
A. A rodeo grounds and race track with concession stands, tourist cabins, and a store and gas station.

Q. Which dude ranch also raised silver foxes and kept a small herd of pronghorn in 1924?
A. The White Grass, just north of the JY Ranch.

Q. What was the favorite Sunday morning horseback destination for dudes of the Bar B C, White Grass, and other nearby ranches?
A. The Chapel of the Transfiguration at Moose. The little log chapel, with its classic view of the Grand Teton out its front window, was built in 1925 of native pine logs. It is still open to the public, all day, every day of the year.

Q. Who was the first couple to be married in the Chapel of the Transfiguration?
A. John and Ellen Dornan, founders of the famous Dornan's bar, wine shop, and chuckwagon restaurant in Moose, on October 11, 1927.

Q. What are the only old-time dude ranches still operating within Grand Teton National Park?
A. The Triangle X and the Moose Head. Both ranches are located on the eastern edge of the park, just a few miles south of Moran. The Triangle X was started in 1927 by John S. and Maytie Turner, and the Moose Head ten years later. While the Moose Head is privately owned, the Triangle X Ranch was sold

to the Snake River Land Company in 1929 and became property of the National Park Service in 1950. It is the longest-running dude ranch in the park and is still operated by the Turner family as a park concession.

Q. Where did the dude ranches get fresh produce for their guests?
A. Much of it came from the farms on Mormon Row.

Q. How many dudes vacationed in Jackson Hole in 1924?
A. The local paper reported 600. Today, approximately one-fourth that number stay at dude ranches here.

Q. In 1927, what did it cost to stay at the Danny Ranch, located on the shores of Jenny Lake?
A. $8 a day. That sounds cheap but it would be more than $200 in today's money.

Q. Who was the Danny Ranch named for?
A. Danny Strange, daughter of one of the original investors.

Q. The Danny Ranch near Jenny Lake is now known as what?
A. The Jenny Lake Lodge.

Q. In 1927 the Double Diamond Ranch, between Cottonwood Creek and Taggart Lake, charged how much for a summer in the Tetons?

A. For $800, a guest received room, board, and activities for the summer—and transportation to and from Philadelphia. Today, one week on a Jackson-area dude ranch will cost three times that much, with some activities such as hunting costing extra.

Q. The Half Moon Ranch, a summer dude ranch for boys and girls, consisted of 27 buildings by 1962. It was located across the road from what prominent park site?

A. It was just across the Teton Park Road from the Taggart Lake parking area and the old park headquarters at Beaver Creek.

Q. The old Double Diamond Ranch at the base of the Tetons became what park facility of today?

A. The Climber's Ranch.

Q. What did the STS dude ranch of the 1920s and 1930s eventually become?

A. The present-day Murie Ranch, home of the late Olaus and Mardy Murie. Located in Moose along the Snake River, the STS had quit operating as a dude ranch when the Muries bought it. The Murie Ranch is now a National Historic Landmark.

Q. What did the name STS stand for?

A. It was a play on the last name of the founders, Buster and Frances Estes. Frances was a young Philadelphia socialite who met cowboy Buster Estes when she stayed at the Bar B C Ranch in 1918. She married Buster and was disowned by her family.

Q. Who were Olaus and Mardy Murie?

A. A husband and wife who came to Jackson Hole from Alaska in 1927. Olaus was a government biologist who was sent here to study the herds of elk. They eventually became renowned conservationists and the authors of several classic books on Alaska and Wyoming.

Q. What present-day conservation organization did the Muries help found?

A. The Wilderness Society. Olaus became president of the society and held numerous meetings at the ranch in Moose.

Q. Who was Olaus Murie's brother?

A. Adolph Murie, who was also a famed biologist and conservationist known for his work in Alaska's Denali National Park.

Q. What unique family relationship did the Muries hold?
A. Adolph and Olaus were half-brothers, and their wives Mardy and Louise were half-sisters.

Q. Another pair of brothers, who first came to Jackson Hole in 1937 and met the Muries, also became well-known biologists. Who were they, and what did they do?
A. Identical twins Frank and John Craighead. They began studying Jackson Hole wildlife in the mid-1940s after WWII, and conducted a study of Yellowstone's grizzlies from 1959 until the early 1970s.

Q. What famous wilderness advocate came to Jackson Hole to visit with his friends, the Muries?
A. Robert (Bob) Marshall, another founder of The Wilderness Society. During the 1920s and 1930s, Marshall published a number of pieces that reformed the policies governing forests and wilderness, eventually causing his name to become synonymous with wilderness. The second largest wilderness area in the lower 48, an area of 1,009,356 acres in Montana, is named for him.

Q. What famous folk singer wrote a song about Mardy and Olaus Murie and came to Moose to sing it to Mardy in person?
A. John Denver, with "A Song for all Lovers."

MOUNTAINEERS

Q. Who were the first mountaineers in the Tetons?
A. Unknown individuals of both pre-historic and more recent American Indian tribes.

Q. Why did they climb the peaks?
A. In their belief system, being in the high peaks gave them

spiritual access to the heavens, endowing them with special powers for healing, hunting, and leading their people.

Q. What evidence do we have of the ancient ones' visits to the mountains?
A. Rock "enclosures" still remain in the Tetons and other western ranges. These enclosures are small, circular sites with rock slabs stood up on end to form a low wall around a flat spot on the ground. The enclosure provided a protected area for fasting and prayer, and communicating with the spirit world through a dream or vision.

Q. Who "discovered" an enclosure at more than 13,000 feet elevation in the Tetons?
A. Nathaniel Langford and James Stephenson, during their 1872 attempt of the Grand.

Q. What was the first major Teton peak to be climbed?
A. The Grand, in either 1872 or 1898, depending on whom you believe. Langford and Stevenson claimed they climbed to the summit in 1872 but left no evidence on the summit nor offered any other definitive proof. William Owen, John Shive, Franklin Spaulding, and Frank Petersen made the first documented ascent in 1898.

Q. What was the occupation of John Shive?
A. He was a local rancher who joined the expedition.

Q. Which two climbers carried on a years-long public debate over which one of them first reached the summit of the Grand?
A. William Owen and Nathaniel Langford.

Q. What job did Langford hold?
A. He was the first superintendent of Yellowstone National Park.

Q. According to Nathaniel Langford, probably via his guide

Beaver Dick Leigh, there was an unsuccessful attempt on the Grand Teton in 1843 by a French trapper. What was his name?
A. Michaud. Although his identity and last name are uncertain, he is believed to be Michaud LeClaire, who was a messenger for the Hudson's Bay Company. Michaud traveled between Fort Hall, Idaho, and Montreal, Canada.

Q. Who claimed to have made the second ascent, also unproven, in 1893?
A. Captain Charles Keiffer, along with Private Logan Newell and Private John Ryan. They were U.S. soldiers stationed at Fort Yellowstone.

Q. How did this ascent come to light?
A. It was described in a letter from Keiffer to William Owen and found in Owen's effects after his death. Keiffer's drawing that accompanied his letter shows a climbing route known today as the technically difficult Exum Ridge, named for Glenn Exum who climbed it in 1931. However, like Langford and Stevenson before him, if Keiffer did make it to the summit he left no evidence of his accomplishment.

Q. Mount Owen was the last major peak to be climbed. Who made the first ascent, in 1930?
A. Robert Underhill, Kenneth Henderson, Fritiof Fryxell (generally pronounced Frit-ee-off Frix-ell), and Phil Smith. Fryxell and Smith, who were seasonal rangers and accomplished climbers, had each made a couple of attempts on the difficult peak in the late 1920s, but had failed to reach the top. Other teams of skilled climbers had also tried and failed. In 1930, Smith and Fryxell teamed up with Underhill and Henderson, two of the leading mountaineers of their day and more technically skilled than Fryxell and Smith.

Q. Just a few weeks later, who made a solo ascent of Mount Owen in one day?
A. Teton climbing legend Paul Petzoldt.

Q. What was the normal climbing attire worn by pioneer Teton climber Kenneth Henderson?
A. A coat and tie, and often a fedora. In his day, there was not any specialized mountain climbing clothing, and climbers just wore their old clothes. Henderson was a banker by trade, so he wore his old business suits. For climbing, he wore rope-soled boots or crepe-soled golf shoes.

Q. Who holds the record for the most first ascents of major peaks in the Tetons?
A. Seasonal park ranger Phil Smith, with six. Four of these were shared with fellow ranger Fritiof Fryxell, who holds second place for most ascents with four (all climbers in a group that make the first ascent of a peak share in the record). Fryxell was a geologist who had studied the rocks of the Tetons for his doctorate in the early 1920s and went on to become a highly distinguished geologist.

Q. Who was the first woman to climb the Grand Teton?
A. Colorado phys-ed teacher Eleanor Davis, in 1923.

Q. What feat did 20-year-old climbing novice Glenn Exum accomplish in 1931?
A. He discovered a new route to the summit of the Grand Teton.

Q. What was Exum wearing on his feet?
A. A borrowed pair of football shoes, two sizes too big, with leather cleats.

Q. Who was Exum climbing with when he went off alone and found the route?
A. Paul Petzoldt, eventually a legend in the Tetons and the climbing world in general. Exum had borrowed the football shoes from Petzoldt.

Q. What did Glenn Exum and Dick Pownall guide to the summit of the Grand in 1952?
A. Two dogs, along with 17 teenage boys.

Q. What breed were the dogs?
A. They were Irish Setter/Black Lab mixes.

Q. In 1954 Glenn Exum guided a man named Pablo Ruthling and his 21-year-old daughter Carmen to the summit of the Grand Teton. What was unusual about Carmen's climb that made it a "first"?
A. She had only one hand (she was born without a right hand) and she climbed the Grand barefoot.

Q. What event interrupted the mountaineering exploration of the Tetons?
A. World War II.

Q. When World War II broke out, most of the Teton climbers entered the military. What division did many of them join?
A. The legendary 10th Mountain Division.

Q. Through the 1950s and 1960s the Teton were home to many of the pre-eminent climbers of the day. What climbing pioneer, who later went on to revolutionize both climbing and outdoor gear, made many of the first ascents of difficult routes in the Tetons?
A. Yvon Chouinard, founder of the Patagonia outdoor clothing and gear company.

Q. What summer housing accommodations did Yvon Chouinard use, years before his business success, when he was climbing in the Tetons?
A. He lived in an abandoned incinerator. During the 1930s, the Civilian Conservation Corps, or CCC, had a large camp near Jenny Lake for the hundreds of young men who worked on the park's trails and buildings. After the CCC left the park in 1942, their remaining facilities were used by climbing guides. Chouinard found that the camp's concrete incinerator made a snug, rainproof accommodation.

Q. What brilliant young Teton climber and guide died on Mount Everest in 1963?

A. Jake Breitenbach, who died under a massive wall of falling ice while negotiating through the Khumbu Icefall.

Q. What happened to Breitenbach's friend and Everest climbing partner, Barry Corbett, also a climbing guide from the Tetons?
A. After Jake's death, Barry gave up his spot on the team that finally made it to the top, figuring he could return and climb Everest another year. But Barry was never able to return—he was paralyzed in a helicopter crash six years later.

Q. What notoriously difficult ski run at the Jackson Hole Ski Area is named for Barry Corbett?
A. Corbett's Couloir, a steep, narrow run that begins with a leap off a high snow cornice.

Q. What Teton climbing pioneer founded the National Outdoor Leadership School (NOLS) and originated the Leave-No-Trace wilderness ethic?
A. Paul Petzoldt, who made his first ascent of the Grand Teton in 1924 at the age of 16. Petzoldt was a member of the first American team to attempt K2, and during WWII he trained fellow troops in the U.S. Army's 10th Mountain Division.

Q. Who is considered to be the first professional climbing guide in the Tetons?
A. Paul Petzoldt, who began taking people up the Grand Teton in the 1920s. In 1924 he made four guided ascents of the Grand.

Q. In 1950, the park established mandatory registration for climbers. How many people registered for climbs that year?
A. 1,000.

Q. How many people registered for climbs ten years later, in 1960?
A. 2,500. That year, there were eight reported accidents and three fatalities.

Q. What is the record for the fastest ascent of the Grand Teton?
A. One hour and 53 minutes, by Bryce Thatcher in 1983. Up to that time, the fastest time was just under four hours. For comparison, most climbers take two days for the ascent, although numerous experienced climbers make the summit in a day.

Q. What is the Grand Traverse?
A. A circular climbing route that begins and ends at the Lupine Meadows parking lot and includes ascents of Mount Teewinot, Mount Owen, the Grand Teton, Middle Teton, South Teton, Nez Perce Peak, and five intermediate summits along the way. The first leg in this grueling climb is a 5,600-foot run (more than a mile) up the east face of Mount Teewinot.

Q. What is the record for the Grand Traverse?
A. 6 hours and 45 minutes, by Rolando Garobotti in the summer of 2000. The previous record was eight hours and 15 minutes by the late Alex Lowe. A normal, fit climber will take six to eight hours just to climb and descend the first peak, Mount Teewinot.

Q. Who had the dubious distinction of being the first recorded climbing fatality in the Tetons?
A. Theodore Teepe (pronounced like the Indian tipi), in August 1925. Teepe was descending a snowfield with his guide, Gibb Scott, after a successful ascent of the Grand when he lost control and slid to his death on some exposed rocks.

Q. What posthumous honor did Teepe receive?
A. The glacier where he died was named Teepe Glacier, and a nearby granite spire was named Teepe Pillar.

Q. What climber was called upon to bring Teepe's body down from the mountain?
A. Paul Petzoldt, who claimed that this incident got him thinking about mountaineering safety. He later developed a system of voice signals for climbers to communicate with, and he taught safety and rescue procedures in his climbing schools and the National Outdoor Leadership School, which he founded.

Q. Who was the first National Park Service climbing ranger in the Tetons?

A. Richard Emerson, in 1950. Emerson was a superb technical climber who pioneered some of the most difficult routes in the Tetons. He had been a member of the Army's 10th Mountain Division, was later a member of the 1963 Everest Expedition, and went on to become a professor of sociology at the University of Washington.

Q. What is the cause of most mountaineering accidents in the Tetons?

A. It is not the actual rock climbing but the traveling over snow- and ice-covered terrain.

Q. What is the cause of most climbing *fatalities* in the Tetons?

A. Falls on rock by un-roped climbers either ascending or descending the peaks.

Q. What is the average number of climbing incidents each year that require a response by park rescue personnel?

A. 120.

Q. What is the average age of men who are involved in a climbing accident in the Tetons?

A. About 36, and most of their accidents occur descending ice or snow.

Q. What is the average age of women involved in a climbing accident in the Tetons?

A. About 30, and their accidents almost always involve falling during a descent on snow.

Q. What peak has the greatest number of climbing accidents?

A. The Grand Teton, because of its popularity. However, the rate of accidents per total number of climbers on the Grand is lower than on other peaks.

Q. What was the overall accident rate for climbers and back-country users between 1950 and 1996?
A. 0.31%. In other words, less than one-third of one percent of climbers and backcountry users get into an accident.

Q. What technical device has greatly increased the number of reported incidents in the past decade?
A. The cell phone.

Q. What is the total number of known climbing fatalities in the Tetons?
A. To date (2009), it is 100.

Q. Who made the first winter ascent of the Grand Teton?
A. Paul Petzoldt, his brother Eldon, and Fred Brown, on December 19, 1935.

Q. What did climbing guide Bill Briggs do in the spring of 1971?
A. He made the first ski descent of the Grand Teton.

Q. What other first ski descents has Briggs made?
A. The Middle and South Teton peaks in 1967, Mount Moran in 1968, and Mount Owen in 1974.

Q. What physical condition did Briggs have to overcome?
A. He has a surgically fused hip. Born without a hip joint, Briggs got by for 30 years with a socket the doctors chiseled into his hip bone when he was 2 years old. In 1961 he had the joint fused and went on to become an extreme skier, mountain guide, and head of a ski school.

Q. Who made the first snowboard descent of the Grand Teton, as well as most of the other major Teton peaks?
A. Stephen Koch, a local mountaineer and snowboarder who guides in the Teton Range. In 2004, Koch attempted to snowboard Mount Everest but dangerous snow and ice conditions forced him to turn back before reaching the summit. He snowboarded a lower route on Everest. Earlier in the expedition, he snowboarded Changzheng, a 24,890-foot peak nearby.

Q. What other snowboarding record does Koch hold?
A. He's the only person to have snowboarded the highest summit on all seven continents.

Q. Koch's snowboarding career almost ended in an avalanche on what peak?
A. Mount Owen. In April, 1998, Koch was caught in an avalanche and carried 2,000 feet down the steep slopes of the peak. He had to bivouac overnight with a broken leg and other severe injuries, and was discovered by the Jenny Lake Rescue Rangers searching for him the next morning by helicopter.

Q. Irene Beardsley, the wife of the late legendary Teton climber and author Leigh Ortenburger, holds a Ph.D. in physics from Stanford and was a member of the first American ascent of Annapurna in the Himalayas in 1978. Among her many "firsts" in the Tetons, what was the most famous?
A. The first all-woman ascent of the notorious North Face of the Grand Teton, in 1965.

Strange Characters

Q. Besides the early trappers and later homesteaders, what kinds of people were drawn to the remote Jackson Hole country?
A. Outlaws.

Q. What horse thief used the valley for his operations even before the first homesteaders arrived?
A. Teton Jackson.

Q. How did his operation work?
A. He stole horses in Idaho, hid them in Jackson Hole, and then drove them to central Wyoming and sold them. While he was there, he stole other horses, drove them back to Jackson Hole, and sold them in Idaho.

Q. What did the Jackson Hole locals think of Teton Jackson?
A. They knew him as a family man and liked him because he didn't steal from them.

Q. What outlaw who lived in a log cabin along Jackson Lake stole horses and robbed tourist stagecoaches in Yellowstone National Park?
A. Ed Trafton.

Q. What robbery record does Trafton reportedly hold?
A. He held up 16 Yellowstone stagecoaches in one day.

Q. What famous western writer modeled one of his villainous bad men after Ed Trafton?
A. Owen Wister, in his novel *The Virginian*.

Q. What gruesome find did a party of fishermen make along the Snake River in 1886?
A. They found the bodies of three murdered German gold miners.

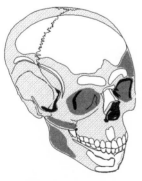

Q. Who committed the murders?
A. A fourth miner, named John Tonnar, who had fled to Idaho.

Q. Who captured him?
A. A local posse tracked down Tonnar and took him to the county seat in Evanston for a trial.

Q. What did the posse prepare as evidence against Tonnar?
A. They cut off the heads of the 3 dead men and boiled the

skulls to show how the men had died. Two of the men had axe wounds to their skulls; the third man was shot in the back. One of the skulls and the bucket used to carry it to court are on display at the Jackson Hole Historical Society and Museum in Jackson.

Q. What punishment did Tonnar get?
A. Nothing. He declared it was self defense and he was released.

Q. What is the name of the site in present-day Grand Teton National Park where the miners' bodies were found?
A. Dead Man's Bar.

Q. What strange character claimed the homestead farthest north in the valley, along the shores of Jackson Lake?
A. John Dudley Sargent, in 1890. Struthers Burt, dude rancher and author who knew most of the characters in Jackson Hole, described Sargent as "a tortured, hampered, damned sort of poet."

Q. What was Sargent known as?
A. He was a "remittance man," a man who was an embarrassment to his wealthy parents and was paid an allowance (or "remittance") to stay far away from them.

Q. What was Sargent's problem?
A. He was mentally unstable, with a maniacal temper.

Q. What did Sargent build on his homestead?
A. A ten-room log lodge that he named *Merymere*.

Q. What other remittance man came to the valley with Sargent and stayed at Merymere?
A. Robert Ray Hamilton, a relative of Alexander Hamilton, the first U.S. Secretary of the Treasury. Hamilton, a lawyer, was leaving behind an alleged affair in the East, and it was widely speculated that he became involved with Sargent's wife at Merymere.

Q. What happened to Hamilton?
A. He drowned on a hunting outing while trying to ford the Snake River on horseback. It was the signal fire alerting searchers to the discovery of Hamilton's body that gave Signal Mountain its name. Locals suspected that Sargent directed Hamilton to the unsafe river crossing, or was perhaps more directly involved in his death.

Q. What other death was associated with Sargent?
A. His first wife, Adelaide, died of extensive injuries that Sargent blamed on a "skiing accident." Sargent was charged with her murder, but the case was dismissed for lack of evidence.

Q. What was his second wife, Edith, known for?
A. Sitting nude in a tree and playing her violin. She had a favorite spruce tree with a deeply curved trunk, overlooking Jackson Lake. The tree where she liked to sit (including a nail where she hung her violin bow) is still there.

Q. What eventually happened to the Sargents?
A. Edith was committed to an asylum, and John later took his own life at Merymere.

Q. What happened to Merymere?
A. It was purchased in 1926 by W. Lewis Johnson, a retired Hoover Vacuum executive. When he died the homestead was bought by Alfred Berol, a pencil company heir, who named it the AMK Ranch. His heirs sold it to the park in 1976 for $3 million, and today the University of Wyoming operates a research center there.

Q. Although none of Sargent's buildings and improvements still exist, his grave remains on the property. What other physical feature reminds visitors of John Dudley Sargent?
A. Sargent's Bay on Jackson Lake is named for him.

Q. How many glasses of beer did Wilford Nielsen, the Teton County Attorney and editor of the local paper, drink in one sitting in 1933?
A. 96. He was trying to drink 100.

Q. What was peculiar about "Uncle Jack" Davis, an early 1900s settler in the valley?
A. He was a vegetarian.

Q. Eccentric homesteader John Dodge was a Harvard graduate and musician. What method did he employ in order to avoid having to cut and carry firewood?
A. He would set a 20-foot log through a window of his cabin and slowly feed it into the stove as it burned.

Q. What skill made Eleanor "Cissy" Patterson, the "Countess of Flat Creek," a down-to-earth person in the eyes of the locals?
A. She was exceptional at cussing—the only woman (or man, for that matter) that stage driver Clay Seaton would let talk to his horses "when they needed talking to." Patterson first arrived in Jackson Hole in the 1920s and stayed at the Bar B C Ranch near Moose. She was the heiress to a newspaper fortune and a Polish countess by marriage. After visiting the area for a number of years, she bought her own ranch on Flat Creek, east of the town of Jackson, and was thereafter known as the Countess of Flat Creek.

Q. The Countess's ranch foreman in the 1940s, Forney Cole, was known for what feat of bravery?
A. While Cole was investigating a beaver dam, he was attacked from behind by a grizzly bear. After realizing what was happening and playing dead for a minute, Forney grabbed a beaver-chewed aspen limb about the size of a baseball bat and laid the bear out cold with one swing to its head.

Q. In the 1930s, members of a spiritual and mystical organization known as "I AM" spent many summer months watching the Grand Teton. What did they expect would happen?

A. The Grand would open up and be full of gold. The "I AM Activity" was started by Guy and Edna Ballard in 1930, when Ballard reported meeting another hiker on Mount Shasta, California, who identified himself as Saint Germain. Guy Ballard was a mining engineer and student of Theosophy whose teachings often revolved around gold mines or mountains filled with gold.

Movies, Arts, and Literature

Q. What famous photographer took the first picture of the classic view of the Tetons from the site of the present-day Snake River Overlook, in 1942?
A. Ansel Adams.

Q. What is the most exotic place where Adams' Teton photograph has gone?
A. It is aboard the U.S. *Voyager II* spacecraft, sent on a one-way trip deep into unknown space.

Q. What year marked the beginning of Hollywood filming in Jackson Hole?
A. 1921, with the filming of *Nanette of the North,* a silent

film. The title was a play on *Nanook of the North*, a documentary on Eskimo life. The original film was lost in a fire and the movie was re-shot in Alaska.

Q. What was the first feature film of Jackson Hole?
A. *The Cowboy and the Lady,* filmed in 1922. Part of it was filmed up Cascade Canyon.

Q. Who was the main actress in *The Cowboy and the Lady*?
A. Mary Miles Minter. She was born Juliet Reilly in 1902, the daughter of a Broadway actress, and began working when she was 5 years old. She made her first feature length film in 1915, and her career grew steadily until 1923, when Paramount Pictures failed to renew her contract.

Q. Why was *The Cowboy and the Lady* Minter's last big film as the star?
A. Minter was accused of murdering director/actor Desmond Taylor, who was found shot to death at his home in California. Minter was supposedly his lover and had sent him love letters. She became one of the prime suspects in his death, but more recent investigation points to Desmond Taylor's being gay and that he was shot by Mary's mother, Charlotte Shelby. Though Minter received several film offers after that episode, she declined them all. She married her milkman and lived in seclusion until her death in 1954.

Q. In what movie filmed in the park did John Wayne make his debut?
A. *The Big Trail.*

Q. What year was *The Big Trail* filmed?
A. 1930.

Q. What was special about *The Big Trail*?
A. It was filmed in color. Although the very first full-length color film, *Cupid's Angling*, was made in 1918, color film wasn't widely seen until *Gone with the Wind* and *The Wizard of Oz* in 1939.

Q. In making the film, what was Wayne reportedly required to do for the first time?
A. Ride a horse.

Q. How much was John Wayne paid for starring in *The Big Trail*?
A. $75 per week.

Q. What nearby town was a "boomtown" during the filming of *The Big Trail*?
A. Moran, at least according to John Wayne. He later said, "There was a place called Moran Camp, on Jackson Lake. It probably had 5 or 6 little shacks when we arrived. We came out with 350 people, and by the time we were through, we had about 500 people working there with a hundred and fifty wagons and horses. We enlarged the place, built cabins and sets, and they ended up with an establishment that is now called Moran, Wyoming. It's a township, I don't imagine there's too many tall buildings out there, but still, we started it."

Q. What were the two films made in Grand Teton National Park in the 1940s in which actor Wallace Beery starred?
A. *Wyoming* and *Bad Bascomb*.

Q. What did Beery do after the making of these films?
A. He decided to stay in Jackson and bought a cabin on the shores of Jackson Lake.

Q. What local business did he buy?
A. The Log Cabin Bar in Jackson. After changing hands and businesses a few more times, the log building was replaced by the present-day Coldwater Creek outlet store. It is located on the south side of the Town Square.

Q. What local protest did Beery get involved in?
A. An armed ride in protest of the 1943 designation of the

Jackson Hole National Monument. Beery fancied himself as one of his Western characters, and he was easily persuaded by a local rancher into joining the protest. It was hoped that Beery's presence would give it national attention, which it did.

Q. One of the local ranchers who accompanied Beery on this protest ride was Cliff Hansen. His family's ranch was previously used as a location for what 1939 film?
A. *Down the Wagon Trail*, starring Tex Ritter.

Q. How did Beery, who starred as a rough cowboy in most of his films, begin his career in Hollywood?
A. As a female impersonator.

Q. What eventually happened to Wallace Beery?
A. He died in April, 1949, at age 63, of a heart ailment. His funeral in Hollywood was attended by more than 2,000 people. He appeared in more than 200 films, which have grossed over $50 million.

Q. Where was the cavalry fort in *Bad Bascomb* located?
A. A façade of the walls, front gate, and guard towers was built on the Square G guest ranch, which was located in the meadow where the present-day Cathedral Group Turnout entices visitors to stop and photograph the Tetons. The Square G buildings were removed in the 1950s.

Q. How did the park's present-day "RKO road," which begins near the Taggart Lake parking area and follows the Snake River all the way to Signal Mountain, get its name?
A. The road was used to access to a huge film set built by RKO studios for the film The Big Sky, in 1952.

Q. How was a raging Snake River created for some of the boating scenes in The Big Sky?
A. The scenes were filmed just below the Jackson Lake Dam, and on cue the dam's floodgates were opened wide.

Q. Who was the star of the film *Spencer's Mountain*, made in

Grand Teton National Park in 1963?
A. Henry Fonda, who was well-liked by everyone in Jackson Hole who met him.

Q. What famous TV series developed from the movie's story of family sacrifice?
A. *The Waltons*. Although *The Waltons* chronicled the lives of a rural Virginia family, it was based directly on the book *Spencer's Mountain*.

Q. Where was *Spencer's Mountain* primarily filmed?
A. Near the Triangle X Ranch, which is between Moose and Moran Junction. The Triangle X is the valley's longest running "old-time" dude ranch.

Q. What local beauty did Henry Fonda court and ask to marry him?
A. Margene Jensen, a cocktail waitress at Wort Hotel's Silver Dollar Bar. Margene had more sense than to run off with Fonda, who was just getting over a previous marriage.

Q. Which one of Clint Eastwood's movies was partially filmed in Jackson Hole?
A. *Any Which Way You Can,* Clint Eastwood's 1980 sequel to his hit film, *Any Which Way But Loose.*

Q. Which Rocky movie starring Sylvester Stallone was partially filmed in Jackson?
A. *Rocky IV.*

Q. What actress played a role in the 1993 movie *The Vanishing*, filmed in Jackson?
A. Sandra Bullock.

Q. What extraordinary scene in *The Big Trail* was actually a mistake but looked planned?
A. While lowering wagons over the Spread Creek Cliffs, one

wagon was dropped and fell approximately 150 feet.

Q. What made actress Marjorie Main in the 1940 movie *Bad Man of Wyoming* seem eccentric to Jackson residents?
A. She juiced various fruits and drank most of her meals, and, due to her fear of germs, she required someone else to open doors for her so she wouldn't have to touch the doorknobs.

Q. Who wrote the novel that the 1951 film *The Big Sky* was based on?
A. A.B. Guthrie, Jr.

Q. Guthrie also wrote the screenplay for the most famous western filmed in Jackson. What was it?
A. *Shane,* starring Alan Ladd.

Q. Where was the town set for the movie *Shane?*
A. On northern Antelope Flats, approximately across the highway (east) and a bit south of the present-day Snake River Overlook on Highway 89-191. If you drive north on the highway from Moose toward Moran and look to your right after you pass the Teton Point Turnout, you will see the area of Antelope Flats where the town stood. At the time there was no highway up the middle of the valley. That road (89-191) was built in the mid-1950s.

Q. Where was the film site of the Starrett homestead in the movie *Shane?*
A. Northwest of Kelly, Wyoming, near the Mormon Row Canal in the middle of the sagebrush. There are no remains of the buildings.

Q. Where was the indoor set of the Starrett homestead?
A. In the gymnasium of the old Jackson High School located on

South Glenwood Street. The site is presently occupied by the Center for the Arts.

Q. At what local hotel did Paramount Pictures reserve 25 rooms for the cast and crew of *Shane*?
A. The Wort Hotel in Jackson, built in 1941 and still in operation today. The Wort is on the National Register of Historic Places.

Q. Why did actor Alan Ladd have to move out of the Wort Hotel and find private accommodations?
A. Cowboy patrons at the Silver Dollar Bar downstairs kept banging on his door at all hours of the night, wanting him to come downstairs and drink with them. They apparently weren't able to separate the actor from the character and assumed he was a hard-living cowboy like them.

Q. Jackson Hole is cattle country, but *Shane* director George Stevens didn't want to use local cattle in the movie. Why not?
A. Stevens, who insisted on authenticity for his films, thought the local cattle were too fat to play the part of a herd belonging to struggling homesteaders.

Q. Where did the cattle in *Shane* come from?
A. Stevens found skinnier cattle in Florida and had them trucked to the Tetons.

Q. During a day off, actor Alan Ladd rode the chairlift to the top of Snow King Mountain. How did he get down the mountain?
A. On a helicopter. The precipitous start of the chairlift down the mountain terrified Ladd and he refused to get on. He also refused to ride or walk down. A helicopter was summoned for him.

Q. Which local lumber store provided building materials for the movie *Shane*?
A. Jackson Lumber, which is still in business.

Q. What remnant of the film *Shane* still stands in Grand Teton National Park?
A. The cabin used for the homestead of character Ernie Wright is just a half-mile east of the Kelly Warm Springs, on the left along the road that leads out of the park and goes toward the Gros Ventre Slide.

Q. Where were the critical stream-crossing scenes filmed?
A. Schwabacher Landing on the Snake River, a few miles north of Moose.

Q. Why didn't the movie premiere at the Teton Theatre in Jackson?
A. The Chamber of Commerce could not afford the $7,000 it would cost to subsidize the premiere.

Q. What child actor in the film *Shane* was often seen in Jackson peering in the windows of the Silver Dollar Bar?
A. Brandon de Wilde (pronounced De-WILL-duh), who played the tow-headed Joey, the kid who worshipped the mysterious gunman. Brandon was looking in the bar at his parents as they partied with the film's stars and crew. Brandon was nominated for an Oscar for his role and went on to appear in many other films. He died in a motorcycle accident at the age of 30 while on his way to perform in a play.

Q. What handsome film star of the 1940s and 1950s was married on a motorboat in the middle of Jackson Lake in 1954?
A. Robert Taylor, who played opposite such stars as Greta Garbo, Vivien Leigh, and Elizabeth Taylor. He later starred in a hit television series, "The Detectives Starring Robert Taylor."

Q. What was Robert Taylor's real name?
A. Spangler Arlington Brugh.

Q. Whom did he marry?
A. Ursula Thiess, billed as the "most beautiful woman in the world." Taylor's first wife was star actress Barbara Stanwyck. Robert Taylor and Ursula Thiess had two children and remained together until Taylor's death in 1969.

Q. What famous actor from the 1930s and 1940s often came to Jackson to hunt and fish?
A. Clark Gable.

Q. Where was Gable's favorite place to stay?
A. Ben Sheffield's Hunting Camp, which was located beside the Snake River just below Jackson Lake Dam.

Q. What actor liked to go to the town of Jackson to gamble after filming in the park?
A. Jack Elam, who acted in *Jubal* (1956) with Glenn Ford and Ernest Borgnine. Elam also appeared in *The Wild Country*, filmed in 1971 in Grand Teton National Park. Elam was known mostly for his roles as villains in numerous Westerns. He was blind in his left eye from a childhood accident and he used his discomforting stare to create an unforgettable bad guy.

Q. What was the Teton location for the filming of *The Wild Country* starring Jack Elam and Vera Miles?
A. The old Hunter-Hereford Ranch, which is located on the eastern edge of the park a few miles north of the town of Kelly. The classic old Hunter barn used in the film still stands today.

Q. What real-life situations did actor Glenn Ford get into in Jackson that reflected his leading man role?
A. He punched a cook at the Wort Hotel who spoke rudely to a waitress, and one night he and fellow actor Charles Bronson whipped a handful of local tough guys in a bar fight.

Q. What Disney film, which aired on "The Disney Hour" in 1960, was shot entirely along the Snake River just north of Moose?
A. *One Day at Teton Marsh*, based on the book by Sally Carrigher. It told the everyday lives of animals such as otters and beaver.

Q. What singer and actor of the 1960s owned a home on the south border of Grand Teton National Park, overlooking the Jackson Hole valley and the Tetons?
A. Robert Goulet.

Q. Who are four celebrities and VIPs that currently own homes in Jackson Hole?
A. Harrison Ford, Sandra Bullock, Dick Cheney, and James Wolfensohn (World Bank president).

Q. Name the U.S. Presidents who visited Grand Teton National Park in (a) 1963, (b) 1971, and (c) 1989.
A. (a) John F. Kennedy, (b) Richard M. Nixon, and (c) George H. W. Bush., Sr.

Q. In 1978 President Jimmy Carter and his wife Rosalyn paid a visit to Grand Teton National Park. What Moose native and Snake River float trip operator took them for a ride on his sailboat on Jackson Lake?
A. Dick Barker, of Barker-Ewing Float Trips.

Q. What former president visited Jackson Hole in the early 1940s and went unrecognized in the town of Jackson?
A. Herbert Hoover. According to mountain guide Glenn Exum, Hoover was visiting friends in the valley and had to have some car repairs done. When he picked up the car, the young mechanic didn't recognize him and asked Hoover to spell out his first and last names, which Hoover obligingly did.

Q. In 1995 and 1996 President Bill Clinton and his family visited the park. What local celebrity did they visit at her home?
A. Moose resident Mardy Murie. Mardy, who was in her early 90s at the time, was known affectionately as the "mother of the American conservation movement." Mardy and her husband Olaus were instrumental in preserving wilderness in Alaska and other states.

Q. What honor did President Clinton bestow on Mardy Murie at the White House in 1998?
A. The Presidential Medal of Freedom.

Q. What important international meeting took place at Jackson Lake Lodge in 1989?
A. The U.S.-U.S.S.R. Pre-Summit World Peace Treaty talks between Soviet Foreign Minister Eduard Shevardnazde and Secretary of State James Baker.

SCIENCE & NATURE

GREATER YELLOWSTONE ECOSYSTEM

Q. What is the Greater Yellowstone Ecosystem?
A. An area of mountainous land centered roughly on Yellowstone National Park. This is not a man-made boundary, but one drawn by biologists to include the species of plants and animals that are ecologically connected to Yellowstone and its surrounding wild country. The GYE is roughly the size of West Virginia, and includes both Yellowstone and Grand Teton national parks, parts of seven national forests, three national wildlife refuges, and lots of state and private land.

Q. After the Ice Ages ended, what was the most important geological process in order for plants and animals to inhabit the valley and the Tetons?
A. The formation of soil.

Q. Why was new soil needed?
A. The melting glaciers had washed away soil over the course of thousands of years, leaving a landscape of bare rock and cobblestones.

Q. How did the first plants find a foothold in the valley?
A. Windblown seeds landed on glacial moraines, which contained good soil.

Q. What small plant was responsible for helping to break down solid rock into soil for plants?
A. Lichen (pronounced "like-en"), a plant that is a combination of an alga and a fungus.

Q. What microscopic life form had to arrive before trees could grow in the valley?
A. The spores of certain fungi. The fungi were needed to "fix" nitrogen in the soil so the trees could absorb it.

Q. How did the fungi spores get here?
A. They were carried on the wind.

Q. Why are the south facing slopes of the hills and buttes bare, while the north facing slopes are tree covered?
A. Windblown soil fell on the north (leeward) sides of the hills. The soil provided nutrients and held enough moisture for trees to grow. The windswept southern slopes had less soil and were (and are) too dry for trees to grow.

BIRDS

Q. How many species of birds have been reported in Grand Teton?
A. 340.

Q. How many bird species are in the U.S.?
A. 925.

Q. How many bird species are in the world?
A. More than 10,000.

Q. What is the largest bird in the park?
A. The trumpeter swan, which is also the largest waterfowl in the world.

Q. How big is the trumpeter swan?
A. Its wingspan may exceed 8 feet and it can weigh 30 pounds.

Q. What was the U.S. population of trumpeter swans in 1933?
A. Only 66 known birds. Trumpeters, which mate for life, were nearly extinct from over-hunting and habitat destruction. During the late 1800s their feathered skins were used to make powder puffs and quill pens. The Hudson's Bay Company in southern Canada exported almost 18,000 swan skins to London during this time. Trumpeter swans were protected in 1918.

Q. What previously unknown population of trumpeter swans was discovered in 1954, bolstering the U.S. numbers to safer levels?
A. About 2,000 breeding birds were found in Alaska. They had been spotted earlier but were thought to be whistling swans.

Q. Breeding pairs of trumpeters were introduced to the National Elk Refuge in 1938, and by 1954 some members of the growing population were nesting at what popular bird-watching site in Grand Teton National Park?
A. Christian Pond, directly across the highway from the Jackson Lake Lodge.

Q. What was Christian Pond named for?
A. Charlie Christian, who homesteaded 160 acres there in 1916.

Q. What do you call a male swan, a female swan, and a young swan of the year?

A. A cob, a pen, and a cygnet, respectively.

Q. What is the present-day population of trumpeter swans?
A. About 16,000, with only about 500 in the Wyoming/Idaho/Montana area.

Q. What is the smallest bird in the park?
A. The calliope hummingbird, a summer resident. It weighs about a tenth of an ounce.

Q. What bird that nests in Grand Teton is also the state bird?
A. The western meadowlark.

Q. Male sage grouse gather at certain locations in early spring to "dance" in order to attract females. What is the area of open ground where they gather called?
A. A lek, from the Swedish word "leka" meaning "to play."

Q. Where is the most unusual location for a lek in the park?
A. On the runway of the Jackson Hole airport.

Q. What small bird arrives high above timberline in the Tetons each spring before snow has melted?
A. The gray-crowned rosy finch. It will nest in a crevice in the rocks and feed on the seeds of small alpine plants.

Q. Which are more common in the park, bald eagles or golden eagles?
A. Bald eagles.

Q. What is the fastest animal in the park?
A. The peregrine falcon, which can dive on its prey at speeds up to 180 miles per hour.

Q. What bird is also called a "camp robber"?
A. The gray jay.

Q. What park bird is the largest owl in North America?
A. The great gray owl, which is almost three feet tall.

Q. What is an easy way to tell the difference between a crow and a raven?
A. When they are on the ground, ravens like to walk and crows prefer to hop.

ANIMALS

Q. How many species of mammals inhabit Grand Teton?
A. 61.

Q. What is the largest mammal in the park?
A. The American bison, weighing up to 2,000 pounds.

Q. What is the second largest?
A. The moose, weighing up to 1,100 pounds.

Q. What is the smallest mammal in the park?
A. The dwarf shrew, at 0.10 ounce.

Q. How far do the park's pronghorns migrate to and from their wintering grounds?
A. 100 miles, following an historic migration route from Grand Teton to the Upper Green River area. They travel via the Gros Ventre River valley just east of the park.

Q. How fast can a pronghorn run?
A. Up to 50 miles per hour.

Q. What park mammal spends eight months of the year in hibernation?
A. The yellow-bellied marmot.

Q. How many quills does an adult porcupine have?
A. 30,000.

Q. How far can porcupines throw their quills?
A. They can't, but the quills are more easily detached when the animals are frightened.

Q. What rare mammal specializes in killing and eating porcupines?
A. The fisher, a large, brown and black, elusive member of the weasel family. Fishers have not been found in Grand Teton but have been seen in Yellowstone. Adult male fishers may grow to 15 or 16 pounds while females are half that size.

Q. What does the pika, a small mammal of the high rocky slopes, spend the summer building?
A. Haystacks of fresh grass that it will eat during the winter.

Q. What is the average maximum lifespan of a wild pika?
A. Three years.

Q. What usually alerts hikers and climbers that a pika is nearby?
A. The pika's alarm call, which varies from a shrill squeak to a high-pitched "hnee" cry.

Q. What other animal lives in high rocky areas and makes a loud whistle?
A. The yellow-bellied marmot, nicknamed the "whistle pig" by old-timers in Jackson Hole.

Q. How many kinds of park mammals fly?
A. Two, the bat and the flying squirrel, although the squirrel

can only glide from a high point to a lower point.

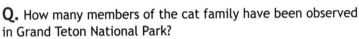

Q. How many of the park's mammal species turn white in winter?
A. Four—three species of weasels and the snowshoe hare.

Q. What rare mammal of the park specializes in catching snowshoe hares?
A. The lynx.

Q. How many members of the cat family have been observed in Grand Teton National Park?
A. Three—the lynx, mountain lion, and bobcat.

Q. How many species of bats live in Grand Teton?
A. Six.

Q. What is the largest rodent in the park?
A. The beaver, at 3 to 4 feet long and weighing 40 to 70 pounds. Beavers continue to grow throughout their lives.

Q. How many members of the deer family live in Grand Teton?
A. Four—elk (wapiti), mule deer, white-tailed deer, and moose.

Q. What was the lowest population reached by bison in Grand Teton?
A. Four, in 1963. At the time, there were 20 bison transplanted from Yellowstone and kept in a 1,500-acre wildlife enclosure near the Oxbow Bend area. Sixteen of those 20 animals were killed in 1963 to prevent the spread of disease, leaving four disease-free calves.

Q. What disease did the slaughtered animals have?
A. Brucellosis, a bacterial disease (*Brucella aborta*) that causes spontaneous abortions in female domestic cattle but does not affect the males. Bison carry the disease but have developed a natural resistance to it. If transmitted to livestock,

the disease causes infertility in females. Controversy exists today over the killing of bison that leave Yellowstone National Park in order to prevent them from spreading the disease to cattle herds. Brucellosis originally came from domestic cattle, but was eliminated in those herds through vaccination.

Q. Today there are wild bison in the park. Where did they come from?
A. In 1968 the sixteen bison in the wildlife enclosure at Oxbow Bend escaped—the four surviving calves plus 12 bison that had been brought in from Theodore Roosevelt National Park in North Dakota. By 2008 this wild herd numbered 1,200 animals.

Q. How many moose did the early fur trappers of the 1800s report seeing in Jackson Hole?
A. None.

Q. Why weren't moose in Jackson Hole in the 1800s?
A. Actually, they weren't here before that time, either. Moose migrated southward from the forests of Canada as the glaciers that once capped the Yellowstone/Teton high country during the Little Ice Age gradually melted and forests began to grow here. During the 1800s the winters were still long and severe, covering what vegetation was available. All in all, there very few moose in the entire Greater Yellowstone area to find their way here.

Q. How old was the oldest recorded moose?
A. 22 years old.

Q. When were moose first found here?
A. They began to arrive (probably from Yellowstone) in the early 1900s. A Forest Service survey in 1912 counted 47 moose.

The Jackson Hole population in 1995 was estimated at 4,000, but by 2006 it had dropped below 3,000 and appears to be on the decline for unknown reasons.

Q. How many native species of fish inhabit the waters of Grand Teton?

A. Nine, including the Snake River cutthroat, whitefish, mountain sucker, mottled sculpin, and various minnows.

Q. How many non-native species are here?
A. Seven, for a total of sixteen fish species in the park.

Q. Of the five trout species found in Grand Teton, how many are native?
A. Only one, the Snake River cutthroat. Rainbow, brown, brook, and lake trout were introduced.

Q. What record fish was caught in Jackson Lake by local woman Doris Budge in 1983?
A. A 50-pound lake trout (mackinaw). Lake trout were introduced to many of the lakes in Grand Teton and Yellowstone years ago before their detrimental impacts on native fish populations were understood. In Yellowstone Lake, for example, lake trout have caused an alarming decline in the population of native cutthroat trout, a decline that affects other park animals that depend on cutthroat trout for food.

Q. How large was the record whitefish, a cousin of the trout, that was caught in the Snake River just south of the park?
A. Four pounds, four ounces in 1977, caught by local fisherman Dennis Jennings.

Q. What park mammal survives by chasing and catching red squirrels?
A. The American marten, commonly called the pine marten. This beautiful golden brown weasel is about the size of a small

house cat, with a golden orange patch on its chest. They are most often observed in lodgepole pine trees, but actually spend most of their time on the ground. They eat more than 100 different kinds of foods, including birds, voles, berries, fruits, and insects.

Q. Coyotes prefer to dig their dens in one certain kind of soil, called loess (pronounced like "less"). Where does this soil come from?
A. It accumulated over the millennia from wind-blown dust and dirt. Almost all the fine dirt and silt of the glacial periods in the Tetons was washed out of the valley by the Snake River, but some of it eventually blew back on the wind.

Q. Why do coyotes like this soil for dens?
A. Because it doesn't cave in on their burrows and dens, unlike loose soils with round glacial rocks.

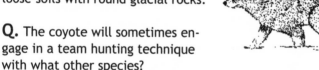

Q. The coyote will sometimes engage in a team hunting technique with what other species?
A. The badger. Coyotes and badgers have been observed hunting together and benefiting from the others' efforts to catch rodents such as ground squirrels. When a badger is digging for a rodent, the coyote will wait nearby and pounce on a rodent that slips past the badger. Likewise, when a rodent escapes from a coyote by hiding in a burrow, the badger will dig it up.

Q. The northern pocket gopher spends most of its life in its underground burrows. How much dirt does an average gopher move in a year?
A. Five tons. One pocket gopher may have 400 to 500 feet of tunnels. The pocket gopher is constantly digging in search of the roots and tubers it feeds on underground. Five tons of dirt is enough to fill an average-sized living room from ceiling to floor.

Q. How big is this earth-moving dynamo?

A. Pocket gophers weigh less than half a pound (6 to 7 ounces) and are only about nine inches long.

Q. How large are pocket gopher colonies?
A. They aren't. Gophers live alone in their own tunnel systems, except for a brief mating period.

Q. What physical features and skills make the gopher ideal for burrow life?
A. The gopher's lips can close behind its teeth while gnawing so dirt doesn't get into its mouth; it has large cheek pockets for carrying food; it has loose skin so it can turn around in tight places; and it can run as fast backwards as forward.

Q. What is the average life span of a pocket gopher?
A. About 18 months.

Q. What is the common name of the bushy-tailed woodrat?
A. Pack rat.

Q. What small pest plagues the park's moose to the point that they may bleed on the snow when they lie down?
A. The tick.

Q. What human disease does the Rocky Mountain wood tick carry?
A. Rocky Mountain spotted fever, the oldest known tick-carried disease. It causes a rash of purplish black spots that first appear on the soles of the feet, ankles, palms, and wrists. If untreated it may lead to delirium and coma. It is curable if treated early.

Q. How many species of reptiles live in the park?
A. Four: three species of snakes and one lizard.

Q. How many of the three snake species are poisonous?
A. None. The three snakes found here are the wandering garter snake, the valley garter snake, and the rubber boa. The climate is too cold for rattlesnakes.

Q. What amphibian was illegally introduced to the park by some unknown individual?
A. The bullfrog. Although the bullfrog seems to be limited to some of the warmer waters of the park, such as Kelly Warm Springs, its presence disrupts the natural ecosystem by pushing out native species of amphibians.

Q. What creature is responsible for killing thousands of lodgepole pine trees in the park?
A. The western pine bark beetle, which has killed about 3 million acres of trees in Colorado and Wyoming. It has reportedly killed 33 million acres of pine forest in British Columbia.

Q. How do beetles actually kill a large tree?
A. Beetles burrow through the bark and make a network of tunnels just underneath the bark. There, the beetles and their larvae eat the soft cambium wood that carries nutrients up the tree trunk, cutting off the tree's food supply.

Q. How does a healthy pine tree defend itself against the beetles?
A. The tree emits a pitchy white resin into a beetle's drill hole, entombing it.

Q. How many years will a lodgepole pine continue to stand after bark beetles have killed it?
A. Anywhere from 7 to 15 years. The dead trees are usually blown over by strong winds.

Q. What park animal climbs above timberline each fall to feast on insects?
A. The grizzly bear.

Q. What insect does it eat?
A. The army cutworm moth, by the thousands. The protein-rich moths gather in large numbers in boulder fields and rocky areas.

Q. Is it true that grizzlies can't climb trees?
A. The cubs can climb, but the claws of adults are not curved enough to dig into the tree bark. All ages of black bears are good climbers.

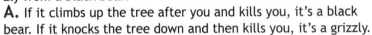

Q. What answer do old-timers tell tourists when asked how to tell a grizzly from a black bear?
A. If it climbs up the tree after you and kills you, it's a black bear. If it knocks the tree down and then kills you, it's a grizzly.

Q. The nut of which tree is prized by grizzlies?
A. The whitebark pine.

Q. How do grizzlies get the pine nuts if they can't climb trees?
A. They find where red squirrels have cached whitebark pine cones and dig up those piles.

Q. How many pumpkin-seed-sized nuts are in a whitebark pine cone?
A. About 35.

Q. How do you tell a black bear from a grizzly bear?
A. A grizzly has a distinct shoulder hump, and its face has a slightly dished profile. The black bear's face has a straight profile, and its rear end often looks taller than its front shoulders.

Q. Are black bears always black?
A. No, black bears range in color from jet black to cinnamon to blonde, and often have a white mark on their chest.

Q. How many bears live in the park?
A. The secretive nature of black bears makes them difficult to count, but there are estimated to be less than 100 bears within the park boundaries. There are many more in the surround-

ing national forests. Grizzly bears, although long absent from Grand Teton National Park, have been migrating south from Yellowstone and the Teton Wilderness to show up in this park. In recent years there have been about 10 individual bears reported.

Q. How many people have been attacked by bears in the park?
A. Only two people have been attacked by grizzly bears in recent years, with no fatalities: one in 2007 and another in 2001. There have been grizzly bear conflicts with hunters in the surrounding national forests and wilderness areas, but no fatalities. There are no recorded fatalities by black bears in Grand Teton, despite several incidents of aggressive behavior by the bears.

Q. Are bears the most dangerous animal in the park?
A. No. More people get charged by bison and moose than get attacked by bears.

Q. Are there mountain goats in Grand Teton?
A. Yes, they are occasionally spotted in the mountains near the southern border of the park. Mountain goats were introduced

years ago to the Snake River Range just south of the Tetons.

Q. How many elk live in Grand Teton?
A. About 3,000.

Q. How many years do elk live?
A. The average lifespan is 12-15 years, but they can live past 20.

Q. What part of an elk was prized even more than antlers by hunters in the early 1900s?
A. The ivory teeth, which are rounded canine teeth.

Q. What were the men called who killed elk for these teeth and sold them?
A. Tuskers.

Q. Who bought the majority of the teeth and used them for jewelry?
A. Members of the Elks Club, a fraternal organization, used them for cuff links, rings, and watch fobs.

Q. How much was a pair of ivory teeth worth on the open market in the early 1900s?
A. As much as $100 for a prime matched pair.

Q. When were tuskers run out of Jackson Hole?
A. 1906.

Q. Who threatened the tuskers with death if they didn't leave?
A. A vigilante posse of locals, including Bill Menor, who operated Menor's Ferry at Moose. For the most part the local people believed in a "live-and-let-live" policy with their neighbors, but the tuskers' deliberate waste of the elk hides and meat triggered a response. Many locals not only relied on the elk for food, but they also were proud of their well-known herds.

Q. What event prompted the establishment of the National Elk Refuge that borders Grand Teton?
A. A massive die-off of starving elk in the winter of 1908-1909. As ranchers homesteaded and fenced off the best grassland for themselves, the wintering elk were forced onto smaller and more crowded grounds, where they ran out of food. Stephen Leek, homesteader and amateur photographer, publicized the elk deaths with his photographs and helped spur Congress into setting aside money for a refuge.

Q. When was the refuge established?
A. 1912. The original refuge was 1,760 acres.

Q. Even after the refuge was established and elk were fed hay in the winter, elk continued to die. What well-known Alaskan biologist was sent to Jackson Hole in 1927 by the U.S. Biological Survey to study the winter elk die-offs?
A. Olaus Murie, who had studied caribou in Alaska and traveled over much of the Arctic. Murie remained a resident of Jackson Hole for the rest of his life, finally settling on a defunct dude ranch near Moose and becoming one of the country's premier conservationists.

Q. What did he discover about the dying elk?
A. The elk were dying from a bacterial disease called "necrotic stematosis," which infected the weak and undernourished animals.

Q. How large is the National Elk Refuge today?
A. Nearly 25,000 acres. Its northern border abuts the southern boundary of Grand Teton National Park.

Q. How many elk winter on the National Elk Refuge?
A. About 6,000 or 7,000.

Q. What is the population of the entire Jackson Hole elk herd?
A. It has ranged from about 13,000 to more than 18,000 animals.

Q. What was the estimated population of the Jackson Hole elk herd in the mid-1800s when the first settlers arrived?
A. About 60,000.

Q. What was the range of elk in North America before the arrival of Europeans?
A. Elk were found from coast to coast.

Q. How much do elk antlers weigh?
A. A large set of antlers on a mature bull could weigh 40 pounds.

Q. Who built the arch of elk antlers on the Jackson Town Square?

A. The first elk horn arch was constructed on the corner of Broadway and Cache in 1953 by members of the Jackson Rotary Club. The other three arches were built as elk antlers became available. Rotary members participating in the 1953 construction included George Lumley, John Wort, Walt King, Jack Francis, Harry Clissold, Slim Lawrence, Joe Jenson, Homer Richards and Cabot Cummings.

Q. What three members of the Canidae family (dog family) are found in Grand Teton?
A. The coyote, gray wolf, and red fox.

Q. Wolves were reintroduced in Yellowstone National Park in 1995. When did they migrate to Grand Teton and successfully den?
A. 1999.

Q. When were wolves eliminated from the area that is now Grand Teton National Park?
A. In the early 1920s. The local cattlemen's association hired a professional bounty hunter to wipe them out.

Q. What was the bounty paid on wolves in the early 1900s?
A. The hunter hired to kill wolves was paid $22 a month plus $62 for a female wolf, $52 for a male, and $22 for each pup.

Q. How much was a cattleman charged to pay for this bounty?
A. Each rancher was assessed 12 cents per head of cattle, and the money went into a fund called the Fish Creek Wolf Association.

Q. How many wolves live in the Jackson area today?
A. About 30-40 wolves in 5 packs.

Q. What is the only bird in Grand Teton National Park that is able to "fly" underwater?
A. The American dipper.

Q. What physical features allow the dipper to forage underwater for insects?
A. It has filmy feathers with a thick down undercoat, a large preen gland that provides it with waterproofing oil, a flap that keeps water out of its nostrils, a transparent membrane (third eyelid) that can cover its eyes, and short stubby wings.

Q. How many species of the weasel family (Mustelidae) live in Grand Teton National Park?
A. Nine—the marten, mink, wolverine, badger, river otter, skunk, and three types of weasels.

Q. How far did a male wolverine, which was caught in the Tetons in 2004 and outfitted with a Global Positioning System (GPS) radio collar, travel in its normal wanderings?
A. In the first 19 days after it was collared it traveled 256 miles to the Portneuf Mountains of Idaho and back. It then went on a 140-mile trek to Yellowstone and back, in one week. At this point, the GPS collar fell off but the wolverine was tracked for the next year-and-a-half by means of a VHF radio implant. It was located in the Gros Ventre, Wind River, and Salt River mountains in Wyoming and in the Centennial Range along the Idaho-Montana border.

PLANTS

Q. How many species of plants grow in the harsh climate of Grand Teton?
A. More than 1,000.

Q. What is the largest and most diverse natural community here?
A. The sagebrush community, with more than 100 species of

plants, covers most of the flat country in the center of the valley.

Q. What is the official flower of the park?
A. The alpine forget-me-not, a brilliant blue, tiny flower that grows at high elevations.

Q. How many species of wild orchids grow in Grand Teton?
A. Seven.

Q. What park plant was highly prized by American Indians as a food?
A. The blue camas.

Q. Which part did they eat?
A. The root bulb.

Q. How was it prepared?
A. It was often roasted in a rock oven.

Q. What two exotic plants have invaded the park and threaten to replace native plants in some areas?
A. Musk thistle and spotted knapweed. While a number of more threatening weed species have found toeholds in the park, musk thistle and spotted knapweed can quickly crowd out native plants. Spotted knapweed came from Europe and Asia and now is the number one problem on western rangeland. Musk thistle, also from Asia, can form dense stands in meadows.

Q. What park animal may be helping the spread of these weeds?
A. The weeds prefer to grow in disturbed soils, so it is believed that bison may speed up the spread of weeds by their habit of wallowing in dust bowls. The bison may pick up seeds on their fur and carry the seeds to new sites.

Q. What did scuba divers discover on the bottom of Jenny Lake in 1984?
A. Dead trees standing upright.

Q. How did the trees get there?
A. The trees were carried into the lake by an avalanche, and the weight of rocks held by the roots caused the trees to stand upright as if they were rooted in the lake bottom.

WILDFIRES

Q. A wildfire in 1974 burned 3,000 forested acres on the west side of Jackson Lake. What was significant about this particular fire?
A. It was the first naturally caused fire allowed to burn under the National Park Service's new Prescribed Burn Management Policy.

Q. What nearby fires in 1988 tested this policy to the limit?

A. The great Yellowstone Fires of '88. Although the fires didn't extend to Grand Teton National Park, they burned large areas in the John D. Rockefeller, Jr. Parkway between Yellowstone and Grand Teton.

Q. When was the most prominent recent fire in Grand Teton National Park?
A. In 1985, when a fire burned the forest near Taggart Lake, right at the foot of the Tetons. A hike on the Taggart Lake Trail gives visitors a first-hand look at forest re-growth.

Q. Why are periodic wildfires good for lodgepole pine forests?
A. Besides clearing out old deadfall, the cones of lodgepoles need the heat of a fire to open up and let their seeds out.

Q. What park bird has its highest local population in the first year after a forest fire?
A. The northern three-toed woodpecker, which mysteriously arrives in unusually high numbers to nest in burned out forests the first spring af-

ter a fire. The most likely reason for their influx is the sudden increase of insects that feed on the dead trees, but no one is sure how the woodpeckers find the burned forests.

CLIMATE

Q. What is the average annual precipitation (moisture from rain and snow) in Moose, where the Craig Thomas Discovery and Visitor Center is located?
A. 21 inches.

Q. What is the average snowfall for the month of December in the town of Moose?
A. 40 inches.

Q. What is the average snowfall in December at an elevation of 9,500 feet in the Tetons?
A. 72 inches, or six feet.

Q. What is the average annual snowfall in the park?
A. 191 inches. The average rainfall is 10 inches.

Q. What was the coldest temperature recorded in Grand Teton National Park?
A. Officially, the coldest was minus 63 degrees F at the Moran ranger station on February 9, 1933. However, an unofficial temperature of minus 63 degrees was widely recorded in the Moose area on January 1, 1979.

Q. What was the hottest temperature recorded in the park?
A. The hottest temperature was 98 degrees on August 19, 1981.

ABOUT THE AUTHOR

Charlie Craighead—born in Jackson, Wyoming—is a writer and film-maker who grew up in a family of biologists. Charlie graduated with a B.S. from Utah State University in 1973 and worked on research studies of grizzly bears, golden eagles, Aleutian Canada geese, and other wildlife before switching full time to photography and cinematography. He has worked for Allied Film Artists, National Geographic, Wolfgang Bayer Productions, Nature, Discovery, and others. His nature cinematography appears in dozens of films on such subjects as the Tetons, Yellowstone National Park in winter, wild horses, the Colorado River, polar bears, and mountain lions.

Craighead's book credits include *Images of Nature: The Photographs of Thomas D. Mangelsen*; *The Grand Canyon: An Artist's View*; *Who Ate the Back Yard: Living with Wildlife on Private Land*; *Never a Bad Word or a Twisted Rope: The Stories of Glenn Exum*; and *Meet Me at the Wort: Legends and Lore of the Historic Wort Hotel*.

His work of the past few years includes filming and producing *Storyteller*, a video about award-winning children's author Jean Craighead George; co-writing a film on the Jenny Lake Rescue Rangers called *Acceptable Risk*; writing a series of eight guidebooks for Grand Teton National Park; and writing exhibit panels for the new Craig Thomas Discovery and Visitor Center in Grand Teton National Park. He is currently producing a film on the Jackson Hole Conservation Alliance. Charlie lives in Moose, Wyoming.

Q. *Are there other fun, interesting books about Wyoming?*
A. *Yes! Look for these books at your local bookstore or call Riverbend Publishing toll-free 1-866-787-2363*
www.riverbendpublishing.com

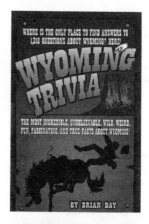

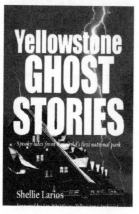

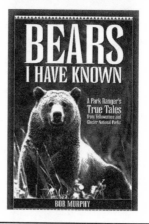